Black Writing
from New Guinea

Asian and Pacific Writing 3

General Editor: Michael Wilding

In this series:

Atheis
by Achdiat K. Mihardja
translated by R.J. Maguire

Tropical Gothic
by Nick Joaquin

Black Writing from New Guinea
Edited by Ulli Beier

Padma River Boatman
by Manik Bandopadhyaya
translated by Barbara Painter
and Yann Lovelock

BLACK WRITING
from NEW GUINEA

edited by **ULLI BEIER**

UNIVERSITY OF QUEENSLAND PRESS

Published by University of Queensland Press,
St. Lucia, Queensland, 1973
This selection © Ulli Beier, 1973

Set in Aldine Roman 12/14 pt.
Printed and bound by
Peninsula Press Limited, Hong Kong
Designed by Norman Birrell

National Library of Australia card number and
ISBN (Cloth) 0 7022 0835 3
ISBN (Paperback) 0 7022 0846 9

To
Albert Maori Kiki
and
Michael Somare

Other books edited and written by **ULLI BEIER**

When the Moon was Big
(New Guinea folk tales) 1972
Words of Paradise
(anthology of traditional New Guinea poetry) 1972
Five New Guinea Plays 1971
Home of Man: The People of New Guinea
(with Paul Cox) 1971
Hohao: the uneasy survival of a Papuan art form
(with Albert Maori Kiki) 1971
Yoruba Poetry
(anthology of traditional poems) 1970
Contemporary Art in Africa 1968
Not Even God is Ripe Enough
(Yoruba Stories, with Bakare Gbadamosi) 1968
Three Nigerian Plays 1967
Introduction to African Literature
(anthology of critical writings from *Black Orpheus*)1967
Political Spider
(stories from *Black Orpheus*) 1969
The Origin of Life and Death:
Creation Myths from Africa 1966
African Poetry
(anthology of traditional African poems) 1966
Black Orpheus
(anthology of new African and Afro-American stories 1964
Modern Poetry from Africa
(with Gerald Moore) 1963, 1968
The Moon Cannot Fight
(Yoruba children's poems, with Bakare Gbadamosi) 1964
African Mud Sculpture 1963
Art in Nigeria 1960 1960
Sacred Yoruba Festivals 1960
Yoruba Poetry
(traditional Yoruba poems, with Bakare Gbadamosi) 1959
Sacred Yoruba Wood Carvings 1957

Acknowledgments

Some of the material in this anthology originally
appeared in *Kovave: a journal of New Guinea Literature*
(Jacaranda Press, 46 Douglas Street, Milton,
Queensland 4066) and in the series Papua Pocket Poets
(available from the University Bookshop,
P.O. Box 5728, Boroko, Papua New Guinea).
John Kasaipwalova's *Reluctant Flame* was published
by Pan African Pocket Poets (Ife, 1971). The glossary
was prepared by Inge Rebe, John Kadiba, & Peter Buak.

Contents

Introduction by General Editor

Asian and Pacific Writing is a series designed to make accessible to English readers some of the world's most exciting and dynamic new literature. The primary concern will be with modern and contemporary work, and the series will contain both translations and work written originally in English, both volumes by single writers and anthologies. The format is flexible so that it can respond to the variety of an area that spans the world's oldest and youngest literary traditions.

As a forum for contemporary writers and translators in Asia and the Pacific, the series will make their work available not only throughout the countries of that area, but to a larger readership in Europe, Africa, and America. It will give expression to an expanding literature outside of the European, Soviet, and American cultural blocs, much of which is barely known beyond its country of origin. Edited and published from Australia, Asian and Pacific Writing marks Australia's developing awareness of her place in Asia. And it marks, too, an international mood of literary exploration, an interest in new forms and new stimuli, a spreading interest in getting to know other cultures, a determination to break down language and other barriers that have prevented literary interchange.

The first volumes are *Tropical Gothic,* a collection of stories by the Filipino writer Nick Joaquin; *Atheis,* a novel by Achdiat K. Mihardja, translated from the Indonesian by R.J. Maguire; the present volume, *Black Writing from New Guinea;* and *Padma River Boatman,* a novel by Manik Bandopadhyaya, translated from the Bengali by Barbara Painter and Yann Lovelock. Further volumes are in preparation.

Michael Wilding

The beginnings of literature in New Guinea

Gavin Souter, the Australian journalist, called New Guinea "The Last Unknown". The romantic title referred, of course, to the fact that New Guinea still had stretches of country unexplored by the white man. In another sense, too, New Guinea could be called the last unknown. For until very recently, it was in fact the last of the colonial countries in which the colonized peoples still accepted their fate without questioning and in which they did not assert their own rights and their own identity in writing.

New Guinea is probably the most anthropologized country in the world, and there has been a continuous flood of books by missionaries, administrative officers and travellers. Yet the New Guineans themselves remained silent and thus, in one sense, they remained unknown to the rest of the world.

All this was changed with Albert Maori Kiki's autobiography *Kiki: Ten Thousand Years in A Lifetime,* published by Pall Mall in London and F.W. Cheshire in Melbourne in 1968.

In his quiet, unassuming way, Kiki was the first New Guinean to tell the world that it was like to grow up in a remote and isolated New Guinean forest; what it was like for a ten year old boy suddenly to be dragged into a mission school; what it was like to be insulted and bullied by Europeans; what it was like to acquire a strange and alien education; and what it was like to wake up to the modern realities of New Guinea and to take part in the shaping of the country's fate.

It was entirely befitting that Kiki should be the first New Guinean to raise his voice: for as secretary of the Pangu Party and secretary of the Port Moresby Trade Union Congress he was in the forefront of those New Guineans who rejected foreign rule, and asserted the right to manage their own affairs.

Australian reaction to his book was interesting and varied: in literary circles and in the universities it received a great deal of sympathetic interest. In New Guinea colonial circles it was received with a great deal of distrust and sometimes hostility. Quite a few people did not believe that a New Guinean had been capable of writing the book. Others thought that it was "aggressive" and "bitter". Although this is probably one of the mildest accusations ever to come from a colonial, Kiki was branded a "radical".

For New Guineans themselves the book was an important breakthrough. It reminded younger New Guineans not only of their own capabilities but of their duties toward themselves and the world. During the next five years we were able to witness a steady flow of New Guinea writing, mostly emanating from the University and Goroka Teachers' College, but also from an ever growing number of secondary institutions all over the country.

New Guinea writing has been simple, direct and often refreshing in its honesty. Writing was not considered as an intellectual entertainment or as a sophisticated exercise, but rather as an urgent task that had to be fulfilled.

The New Guinea writer is a committed writer who believes that he serves society in the following way:

Throughout the last hundred years New Guineans have been written about by outsiders and the image of their countrymen presented to the world has been largely a distorted one. New Guinea writers now want to tell their side of the story. By and large, they are doing this without much rhetoric and with a surprising amount of objectivity.

As New Guineans they wish to define what this new identity is: how much do they owe to the foreign culture that was imposed on them? And to what extent are they still part of the tribal culture they have been educated away from?

There is a great sense of urgency in this writing. The young authors know that their various cultures in their purer forms will not last long. Many University students from the coastal areas only know their own culture from hearsay: their fathers still experienced the culture intact, but they themselves grew up in an emasculated world. Some of the highland students on the other hand, still went through initiation rites in their villages before coming to the University. In both cases there is the desire to capture life in a New Guinea village as they have experienced it. There is a strong feeling among young New Guinea authors that there is a poetry and dignity about this life which outsiders have not been able to see.

Such stories as "Growing up in Mailu" or "Spare that Bird" convey a kind of tenderness that foreign writers have totally missed in their descriptions of New Guinea village life. The poetry of Kumalau Tawali suggests a purity and delicate beauty which could not be captured even by the most sensitive scholar's prose.

The conflict with Western cultures is also powerfully portrayed in this volume. The delighted and alarmed sense of wonder in the "Old Man in the Balus". The alarming sense of destiny in "Man on the Moon" and the intellectual agony in "Disillusionment with the Priesthood".

Only quite recently has there been a militant element in New Guinea writing. "He took the Broom from Me" is a rare example of real bitterness in New Guinea writing. It is a sentiment that will find growing expression as the political situation grows tenser.

The only work of New Guinea literature which so far can be seen forming part of the wider scene of Third World nationalism is John Kasaipwalova's poem "Reluctant Flame". This poem is a spectacular outburst of passion, with echoes of Aime Césaire and the negritude movement but with a human warmth and New Guinean imagery that are entirely the author's own. It is, at the time of writing, the most sophisticated piece of writing to have come out of New Guinea.

Ulli Beier

AUTOBIOGRAPHY

JOHN KADIBA

Growing Up in Mailu

I was born on Koitaki rubber plantation near Sogeri. The first image that impressed itself on my mind was miles and miles of rubber trees, planted in monotonous, regular lines. They are tall trees, with straight stems and their branches tend to point towards the sky. The plantation was kept free of any undergrowth, but once a year, when the trees shed their leaves, the ground would be covered with red and orange leaves. As a small boy I used to go and look for the brightest leaves under the bare trees, with their whitish, irregular branches. When the rains came, the trees sprouted new leaves which shone very bright when the sun caught them. Gradually they would turn into a dark green.

My father had come to the rubber plantation as an ordinary tapper, but was later promoted to be an overseer and put in charge of a small plantation. He was a native of Mailu, but had left his native village and gone to look for work almost immediately after his marriage. Three of his children were born on the plantation: Jimmy the eldest was born when the first bomb was dropped on Port Moresby. I came just after the war and Susan arrived three years later.

The plantation was a lonely place. There were no other families living near and we had no other children to play with. Every morning we watched the same routine of rubber tapping. Each labourer had a certain number of trees allocated to him. First he would go along the line of trees, tapping them about three feet above the ground and tying a little cup to them. Slowly the milky liquid would drip into the cup along the V-shaped cuts on the tree. When the labourers had finished with the tapping they would return to the beginning of their lines and collect the rubber in large buckets. By midday they carried their buckets to the factory for processing. Each man carried two buckets which dangled from two ends of a long stick that was placed across his shoulder. It was a dirty job — their *laplaps* were stained with clogged rubber.

On Saturdays everybody came to collect their rations: rice, tobacco, meat, flour, washing soap and kerosene. Father lined them up early in the morning for checking. Sometimes he found one of them missing:

"Kongi he go where?"

"Em i sik"

Father would have to check up on this later. For the time being he told the rest:

"Yu pela i wokim gut na baimbai yu kisim skel bilong yu. Yu harim?" They would shout "yes", receive their ration and be dismissed to work.

The days on the plantation were much the same. But there was one morning I shall never forget. When we woke up we beheld a strange sight: the dark leaves, the ground, the roof of our house had all been covered by a fine white dust.

"Mother," we shouted, "where did this sand come from?"

My mother was equally puzzled, but she wanted to give us some kind of answer:

"It's your brother Jimmy, who's on holidays in Mailu — he is sending you all this sand."

"Is the sand at our village white?"

"Oh yes," she said. "All along the beach the sand is white. But of course you can't know — you have never been to the sea."

"And — and how did Jimmy send it, Mother?"

"Well," she said, "he put it in the palms of his hands, blew it up, and the wind carried it here."

"He is a good brother, isn't he?"

"Yes," mother said and started to cook rice for our breakfast.

Later as we were squatting on the mat eating our breakfast with spoons or fingers, Father came in from his first plantation round. I was really disappointed when I learned the real explanation of the white sand from him. "Lamington mountain blowed out last night," he said.

"Where is Lamintoni mountain, father?"

Father pointed to the north east and said: "A long way away, behind those mountains there."

During the next few days we heard more and more stories of people being killed and houses being wrecked by the volcanic eruption. One story spoke of a white man who had been hurled up in the air with his jeep and landed on top of a tree, jeep and all.

The first heavy rain washed all the white dust away.

My parents had no education, but on the plantation they were removed from village life and learnt some new ways of living from the European plantation manager. Mother learned to make her own dresses and skirts. For us she made little shorts or *piripous* — as we called them — with braces that tied diagonally across chest and back. Both our parents spoke Motu and Pidgin fluently. They also knew Hula and they had picked up a little bit of English. Such words as: go, come, good, bad, naughty boy, silly girl, good morning, good evening, hello . . . were often used by them though they pronounced them with little ease. We children understood these few words and phrases. We could not express abstract ideas in English, but we knew how to name spoon, pot, pan, plate, knife and fork. My parents took some pride in such knowledge and even gave us European names: Jimmy, John and Susan — names that were quite unknown back home in the village.

My parents were most anxious that we boys should go to school, as early as possible. The subject was often discussed at home and finally my father arranged with the pastor at Sogeri that we should go to the L.M.S. Primary School there. It was arranged that we should stay with the pastor and only come home for weekends.

One Sunday morning my mother put all the spare clothing and *piripous* into a small hand bag and Father took us to the pastor. It was painful to hear Mother say good-bye to us:

"*Aioni* John, *Aioni* Jimmy. You must behave well and

listen to the one who teaches you. *Aioni* — look after your bodies!" I looked back at Mother over my shoulder, then walked ahead of Father and Jimmy with my eyes fixed on my toes. After two or three hours' walk we arrived at the mission station. Father met the pastor and addressed him in Motu:

"*Namo?* — good?" he said offering his hand.

"*Namo herea* — very good" replied the pastor.

"These your children?"

"*Oi be* — Yes. This is Jimmy Kadiba the big one, that is John Kadiba the little one. They are at your hands. If they do wrong, you know what to do with them."

"Do not think about that. They'll be all right."

When all arrangements were made, Father said good-bye to us and turned to walk home. We saw him disappear behind a corner of the road. Already my throat was vibrating, the trees around me were becoming blurred. We walked upstairs and the pastor went to the kitchen to fetch us a drink. No sooner was he out of sight, than I slipped out of the house and ran after my father. Jimmy got confused by my sudden flight and followed me somewhat reluctantly. I ran, crying, as fast as my small-boy feet could carry me. I did not want to stay away from home. I had never been away from my mother before. I caught up with my father after about a mile. The old man stood speechless and looked at me solemnly. I did not dare to say anything, I just stood there, rubbing my eyes with the back of my hand. Father said nothing. He walked straight back to the mission. I understood from his very silence that I had hurt him deeply. When we reached the Mission station he apologized to pastor for my weakness and shameful behaviour. Then he picked up our belongings and walked slowly home. Mother was bewildered: "What happened, why are you all back again?" Father looked at me and said: "It was that silly John. He could not stay away." My mother abused me thoroughly — then she sat down on the mat beside father on the verandah. They were very silent that day. I could not understand, of course, that I had shattered their simple dream. From then on, whenever I did something wrong, my mother would say: "So that's why you did not want to go to school, because you wanted to be naughty at home!"

When I was seven years old my father decided to return to Mailu. He had been away for over twenty years. They had almost forgotten the village way of life. They had no house in Mailu and no garden. Father's older brother gave us half of his own *madava* to plant on, because it takes a long time to clear a virgin piece of land. Father had to fell trees, clear undergrowth burn the *oioi* — that is the as yet uncultivated garden — in order to prepare it for the planting of taro, yam, bananas, sweet potatoes, sugar cane and paw paw seeds. It took many weeks before the *oioi* had been turned into a proper *tako* — a cultivated food garden.

We boys were not expected to work in the garden — it was a girl's job. But we went along sometimes at harvest time, which came when the leaves of the vegetables turned yellow, red and brown. Sometimes all these colours were represented in a single leaf!

While the preparation of the garden was going on, my father also built us a house. *Bedira* trees were cut — the hard red wood was suitable for the houseposts. The *goniga* palm was cut up for floor boards. Its tough, fibrous wood could not be attacked by white ants. The roof was woven from sago leaves and the walls from sago bark. The women were mainly involved in weaving the roof — most of the work was carried out by men. It took about two moons to finish the house.

Meanwhile I got to know the village children. I had never known so many children before. I must have looked like a real stranger among them, because I was the only child wearing clothes. But we soon made friends. I was taught a game called *modiu* that was to prepare me for hunting expeditions. For this game the swollen root of a banana is sliced into the shape of a wheel. There were two teams, ten boys lined up on either side. One side would roll the *modiu* across the field. The other side had to try and shoot it with their spears. This game was meant to teach us how to throw a spear accurately at a running pig.

"*Aiesade*" — coming! we shouted as we rolled the wheel across. "*Godagoda*" they would exclaim in triumph when they hit it.

One day a boy was hit in the leg and started screaming. Blood flowed from his leg and we all ran to hide in the bush to avoid the anger of his parents and ours. From our hiding places we could hear his mother yelling:

"Oh you children, you would die playing this bad game. Come here and let me see you. You old little children, who would die of playing!"

But as soon as the woman's anger had cooled down we continued with the game.

Soon Karau, my cousin, took me on my first real hunting expedition. We were six boys and six dogs. We held a spear each and followed closely behind the dogs. The dogs keep their noses to the ground, sniffing for scents. They took us several miles through the forest and across a mountain, before they showed signs of real excitement. I was lagging slightly behind and when I heard the wild barking, I wondered what the dogs had cornered: a cassowary? A pig? A wallaby? There was no path here, each of us had to find his own way through the thick jungle, following the noise. When I reached the place, Karau was already there, his spear held high to kill the huge boar that had been rounded up by the dogs. But the dogs were so close he did not dare to shoot. The boar was furious. It attacked the dogs and ripped open the side of one of them. Karau had to call the dogs away, in order to be able to throw his spear:

"*Ai, ai, ai — Taiga ai — Dimuda ai — ai ai ai!*"

As soon as the dogs were clear Karau thrust the spear deep into the boar's side. We came out from behind the trees where we had taken cover, shouting *godagoda!* The boar howled in dizzy agony, then became silent, jerked, jerked again and lay still, dead. Blood poured from its side.

We tied its feet and suspended it from a pole, about three feet from the ground. Then we covered it in twigs, set fire to them and thus singed off the bristles. Then we cut it up and wrapped the pieces in leaves, ready to carry home. But it was the custom to eat something before reaching home. The dogs were given the intestines. We baked the heart, the kidneys and the tongue for ourselves.

When we got home at dusk, the pig was shared out between several families. It was much too big to be eaten by one family alone.

A favourite game was story telling. We sat around on moonlit nights, listening to older boys telling us stories. The first legend I heard was about the coconut and how it came to our village:

There were two girls. The elder was called Mudi and the younger Arupa. One day they went to fetch water. When they were filling their pots, the younger girl saw a cucumber floating down the river. Both girls left their pots and raced to get the vegetable.

Arupa roro	Arupa swam
Mudi roro	Mudi swam
Arupa roro	Arupa swam
Mudi roro	Mudi swam
ee Mudi	until Mudi
ma kapurika	got the
evasia	cucumber

When they reached the shore Arupa said to Mudi:

"Friend, cut the cucumber and let us eat it."

"No, we must take our water pots to the village first," said Mudi. They returned home and put the pots away into their proper places. Then Arupa said again:

"Sister, now let us cut the cucumber and eat it."

"No, we must sweep the room first," said Mudi.

When they had finished sweeping the younger sister said once more:

"Now we have put the pots away and we have swept the rooms. Let us cut the cucumber then and eat it."

"No, we must sweep under the house first."

When they had done this work Arupa said to Mudi:

"Now we have put away the pots, we swept the rooms, we

9

swept under the house — let's eat the cucumber now."

"No. You must go and play with your friends first. When you come back, we'll eat it."

So Arupa went to play with her small friends. When she returned she said to her sister:

"I have played with my friends. I have come back. Cut your cucumber and let us eat it."

"Oh friend, while you were playing, I cut open the *kapurika* and I found it was not good for eating, so I threw it to a pig and the pig ate it."

Arupa started to cry. She knew that Mudi was telling a lie. She wept and wept. Her parents returned from the garden and tried to stop her crying, but she could not. She cried and cried until her grandmother arrived from the garden:

"Why is Arupa weeping?" she asked.

When she heard the whole story she put Arupa on her back and carried her back to the garden. Then she placed Arupa down in the garden where the cucumbers were many. Arupa ate and ate, and ate. Her stomach grew big and big and big. It was time to return home. Arupa could not walk on her own feet. Grandmother tried to lift her on her back, but she could not. Arupa had become too heavy. So grandmother placed her between some banana trees and covered her with banana leaves. She wanted to come back the next day to get Arupa.

At night, a man-eating spirit came along and smelled his prey. He looked round the garden and found his meat. He tied her hands and feet and put her on his shoulder and went away. Next morning the man-eater and his wife prepared to boil Arupa alive. They put her in a pot, made fire and then left to get water. Arupa broke the strings that tied her arms and legs. Then she passed waste matter and water in abundance into the pot and quickly climbed up a palm tree. When the couple returned, they found that their meat was overcooked and that not a single bone was left.

"You should have stayed back to look after the meat," the wife said to her husband. However they were hungry and they began to eat the soup. Then they heard a song from a nearby palm tree:

| *Ina buri isiisi* | You are eating waste matter |
| *Ina ea isiisi* | You are eating urine |

"I think I hear a bird's song," said the husband.

Ina buri isiisi
ina ea isiisi

The couple ran out of the house and found Arupa sitting on top of the palm.

"Our food is up there," said the husband. "We have been eating her waste matter and urine."

"How did you get up there?"

"My head downward and my bottom upward," Arupa replied.

The couple tried as she said, but they could not climb the tree. They asked Arupa again:

"How did you get up there?"

"My head first, my bottom last."

The man began to climb the palm tree and his wife followed.

Arupa had sharpened the spines of the palm leaves with a shell. The man-eater was about to place a hand on the lowest branch, when Arupa threw a sharpened branch into his right eye. The man-eater let go and fell, carrying his wife with him. As they writhed in pain on the ground, Arupa quickly came down and cut off their heads. Then she tied the two heads on both ends of a pole and carried the pole across her shoulders, back to the village. As she entered the village, she sang:

Emegi ioro isana	man's head first
emegi ioro deni	man's head last
oro mila	
oro mila	
wui!	

Her grandmother heard the song and told the children who were playing:

"Hey little ones! Keep quiet for a while. I want to listen to that voice. I am hearing."

Emegi iroro isana
emegi ioro deni
oro mila
oro mila
wui!

"I heard a voice like Arupa's" said the grandmother and ran to meet her. She hugged her and cried.

Arupa buried the heads under the house. A few days later shoots appeared on the spot and they grew into tall trees that produced coconuts.

That's how the coconut came to Mailu. And even today, when you look closely at a husked coconut you can recognise the eyes and mouth of the man-eater.

* * *

In the third year of our stay in Mailu, in the month of July, my mother became very ill. She was expecting twins, but the month for her to give birth had already passed and every one in the village was worried.

Mother had always been active and lively in her way of doing things. I remember her always bright, when she was talking and walking. But now she was sad and she moved slowly. She was not the same mother. She knew that people in the village were worried, and she too became worried and afraid. Some afternoons when we sat around her she looked at us and said: "Children, what will happen to you all, if I go? How would others treat you? Would Father have time to look after you properly?" But all this time Father went about his work as usual and paid little attention to the village people's talk.

There was no hospital nearby to which we could have taken her, where she could have been looked after by nurses. But in the meantime people began to wonder why mother had not given birth at the right time. Many people thought that because she was the only woman who had gone to a European place and because she owned many things other women did not have, she had been looked at with evil eyes. Jealous women, so people believed, had bewitched her.

In the end some of her relatives sent for the witch doctor, who lived in a neighbouring village, so that he could exorcise whatever evil thing was stopping Mother from delivering. The witch doctor arrived two days after he received the notice. He was a short man with dark skin and with feathers of wild and domestic birds stuck in his bushy hair. He entered the room in which Mother was resting. A dirty old canvas bag was hanging from his shoulder. He stopped and looked at Mother. Then he went up to her and knelt beside her. He opened his bag and the rich smell of aromatic herbs came out of it. He took out some dry leaves and twigs and chewed them into a brown pulp. Then he put his mouth against Mother's and uttered some words which I did not understand. While Mother sat motionless he performed his magical act. After a while he stood away from Mother. With some effort and looking as if he was about to lose his consciousness, he pulled out a yard long strip of cloth from his mouth. It was said that he had extracted it from Mother's stomach and that it had been placed there by the witches in order to punish her, because she had many good clothes that other women did not possess.

The next day the witch doctor took Mother to a nearby creek where she was to wash off the evil that had been cast upon her. Supported by two women she reached the river. There the witch doctor cut two sticks and placed them across the banks of the narrow creek. He tied some fresh leaves on them which just touched the surface of the water. Mother was then instructed to swim under the sticks, following the current of the river. The current was meant to carry away the evil on Mother's body. Then the doctor was paid and returned to his village.

Three days after the magician had gone Mother gave birth to the twins. At first all was well, but on the second day Mother became very weak. A message was sent to her relatives who arrived from a nearby village on the same day. For the next two days the village was very quiet. The children were not allowed to play. The adults went to the garden very early in the morning and hurried back home as soon as they could — expecting the worst. On the third night Mother had little strength left. Throughout the night all her relatives sat around her. Twice Father prayed that Mother might have rest and peace. He understood clearly now that Mother was to leave us soon.

Two fires were lit in the front and the back of the house. The old men and we children sat around these fires. The men smoked and I was thinking: "Will Mother live or will she go? If she goes — I will not see her face again — never hear her voice." I turned my face away from the fire so that others would not see my tears. The night seemed long. Before the first cock crowed Mother gained a little strength to talk. She asked for her children to be brought up into the house. She was leaning against Father and as we came close to her she looked at us and said: "Jimmy, John, Dibai, Naomi, Susan . . . my children . . . my children. . . ." She said nothing more to us. She turned to our father and said: "Take me down stairs." But he would not allow her. Then she turned to my uncle and said again: "Take me to the ground." Uncle did not move. Mother wanted to see the street and look around during the last minutes of her stay. My father and uncle both knew this was a clear sign that she would leave us soon. Father prayed again and the first cock crowed and Mother drew her last breath. Father said to her: "Good-bye, we shall never see you again." The relatives who had been weeping quietly now cried loudly. And the women all called out at Mother:

"Come back friend . . . come back . . . "

"Oh, you never said a harsh word to your friends . . . why have you left us!"

"Wake up and cook breakfast for your children . . . they are hungry . . . can't you hear . . . wake up . . . "

"You are sleeping too long . . . the sun is up already . . . wake up and carry your basket to the garden . . . wake up . . . "

"Why have you left your children . . . don't you love them?"

While some continued to weep softly, others sang the *damorea,* the traditional mourning song in which my mother's good deeds were recalled.

The morning air was still and dull and the sun was covered by clouds. The village people gathered round the house. My mother's red-haired uncle led off a group of men to dig her grave. My father was too exhausted to help them. The women dressed Mother for burial. They combed her hair and anointed her with coconut oil to make her face shine. They put on her favourite white dress — the one she had made at Koitaki and that she had always worn for service. Her body looked very pale, but she looked fresh like a living woman. Her eyes were closed but she seemed to be smiling. The sun was getting high and her brother came in and announced: "The grave is dug and she must now be buried. She is a Christian woman — *Ekalesia avesa* — and she must not sleep here long." They took her out on the verandah and everybody saw her for the last time. She was wrapped in two blankets and three mats and she was carried to the burial place by four men. As she was lowered gently onto the timber floor of the grave Susan, who was three years old, suddenly burst out weeping. For the first time now, as we dropped the earth into the grave she had become aware of the loneliness which we, the older ones, had already felt.

When Mother's grave had been levelled and we walked back to the village we felt even sadder than when her body was still with us. I looked back at the grave. I thought that the dark patches of clouds in the sky were sheltering Mother from the heat of the sun. I could picture her vividly in my mind: her small face and bright eyes, her thick dark hair. Her complexion was light and whenever she wanted to look bright she rubbed herself with coconut oil. She parted her hair in the centre, brushing it to both sides. She moved in quick steps and never gave the impression of being tired.

Reaching the house now I heard the cries of the twins,

who were being looked after by the woman next door. It was painful to think of her children being nursed by another woman. In the house everything reminded us of her: her cooking pots, her garden basket. For days I tried to avoid the garden — the taros and yams she had planted, the little hut in which she rested.

Father tried to recall us back to life as soon as we reached the house. "We are late, children! You must help me cook the food. Oh — we have no coconut. Jimmy go to your aunt and ask for a coconut. Then scrape it quickly. Naomi, you come and help me to peel the vegetables and you two boys, John and Dibai — go and fill the bucket with water from the river."

The following week Mother's and Father's relatives began to prepare for the funeral feast. Every day the women came and brought more yams and taros, bananas and sweet potatoes. A special hut was built to store all the food which was piled up on its floor of narrow wooden sticks. The feast was to be held on the Sunday. My father's kinsmen killed six pigs and gave them to my mother's relatives. This was considered to be the last instalment of the bride price. Mother's relatives singed off the bristles from the pigs and cut them to pieces. In the meantime the women and children divided all the bananas and other vegetables and heaped them up in six large piles in a straight line. Four of these *dubus* were for the four family clans. The other two were intended for visitors and mourners from other villages. The uncooked pig meat was also divided up and placed on top of the six *dubus*. The women hurried to the river to carry water, getting ready to cook their share. The sun was beginning to go down and the villagers who had come from afar got impatient.

"Hey! Hadn't you people better hurry up? We must get back to our villages before dark."

But those who were responsible for allocating the food were still trying to make up their mind on who should get the last of the boars' heads.

"Who should have it?" my uncle asked.

"There are the people from Ori and those from Geagea.

The people from Geagea are good people, but those from Ori have a reputation for witchcraft."

I thought he would have preferred to give the head to the Geagea people. But in the end he thought it wiser to give it to the visitors from Ori.

At last the names of the different groups were called out:

"People of Ori — come and collect your *dubu.*"

"Geagea people! This is yours" and so on. The people set out for their villages and their friends gave them final parting gifts: hunting dogs, armshells, clothes or money.

The village was quiet again. Everyone went home to cook his own share of the food. In our house, my father addressed our relatives, thanking them for their help and sympathy.

"I thank you for the feast you have made in memory of these children's mother. I am not asking you to make another feast this time next year, for it will be very hard work for you. All I ask of you is to help me look after these small ones she has left behind."

It was the custom in Mailu to repeat these funeral feasts every year, but my father was a Christian and the Missions had discouraged this custom.

The biggest problem of my father's was to find homes for the twins. In the end they had to be separated: the boy was taken to the mission station and was brought up by Reverend and Mrs. Bache. The girl was taken away by the medical assistant. Now — eleven years later — the boy, Ravu, is living with my father. But the girl grew up without knowing her family. I have not seen her since she was two weeks old.

My father had intended to return to the plantation in Koitaki after three years in Mailu. But when Mother died he could not face the idea of returning to the place where he had lived with her when they were a newly married couple. And so his sorrow has made him stay in the village ever since. On the day of the funeral feast Father promised never to marry again. And he has kept his promise to this day.

MAURICE THOMPSON

Nightmares

Out of the blackness he came. I trembled. His eyes were red, glowing like the evening fire. His skin was wrinkled and grey, his nails were long and pointed like a hawk's claws. His nose was large and bold. A grey, wavy bunch of hair hung from his head, right down to his skinny feet. I knew he was an old one of the *Sangalengale* my mother used to tell me about. For a moment I just stood there, my feet paralysed. Then I let out a scream, calling *"Tete, Teteeee, Teteeeee!"* and fled. But mother was nowhere to be seen. I looked over my shoulder and saw the *Sangalengale* coming close behind. I stopped abruptly: I had come to the edge of a cliff. I peeped over the edge, but could see only blackness. I panicked and jumped up and down as the *Sangalengale* approached with a sinister smile, baring his spacious, sharp teeth. Then I saw a root hanging over the edge of the cliff. I started to climb down as fast as I could, but he was climbing after me. I kicked and screamed. I shook the root, trying to jerk him off. Then something happened: the root snapped. It was a long fall. I prayed anxiously:

"Please, *Supe*, you make it so I fall on a river, so I won't die. *Superi*, my *Tete*, she will feel very bad. Please, *Supe*, from now on I will . . . "

Klomf, I crashed on the hard ground.

"Awi, Lord, why did you let me die?"

I thought about my mother, how she would mourn over me. The whole village would weep over my dead body. Relatives and friends from the islands of Emou, Tongoa, Nguno and Efate would come over to cry over me. My body would be washed, clothed and covered with mats. The bell will be struck at intervals: ding, ding . . . ding, ding . . . ding,

ding . . . ding, ding . . . I shall be lifted up, but mother will cling to me, trying to stop them from taking me out of the house. At the cemetery they'll dig a small rectangular hole I'll be lowered into it and a church elder will sprinkle earth over me and say: *Namotamota poki namotamota.* As they shovel the earth down, my mother will cry out again, not wanting them to cover my body. Poor mother. I would come at night to watch them, but they would not be able to see me or hear me or feel me. I cried louder and louder and then I heard a voice, the familiar voice of my father:

"What makes you want to cry? Don't you see that all of us still want to sleep?"

I heard my mother leave their room and to come to me. It was useless now to cry, but I continued to cry so she would come. She said:

"What is it that makes you cry?"

"Oh, *Tete,* I thought that . . .", but I did not dare to mention the *Sangalengale.* I did not want to go to sleep for fear of seeing him again. I looked at the limestone wall and gave a start: there was the picture of a man with a nose like *Sangalengale.* Papa had told me that his name was de Gaulle and that he was a very big man.

If I really died, I thought, I would haunt my family for five days. On the fifth day I would return to the cemetery and there live under the ground among the dead. Later my parents would join me when they died. There, deep down below the surface we would all stay until judgment day, when we all go to paradise. But Papa had once told me that little children, if they were really good, would not have to wait till judgment day. They could go straight to heaven to see Jesus.

When the noisy singing of the birds had died down, I heard my mother open the door to prepare breakfast in the kitchen, a few feet from the sleeping house. Then the melancholy sound of the church bell made me jump out of bed. Somewhere a dog, stimulated by the bell, began to howl. The bell did not ring at intervals but continuously, because it did not summon a dead person. The living were being called to early Sunday service. I sighed. This was Sunday morning and I would not be able to play marbles or catch little fishes on the coral reef at low tide.

At breakfast my father said:

"You know your questions and answers for today?"

"It is very soft. It is not hard at all."

"I did not ask that it is hard or it is soft. You can say it and not looking at the book?"

"I can say it and not looking at the book."

"You try to say it and I shall try to hear."

"Who is man the first? Man the first is Adam, but he did wrong, and *Supe* chased him away from the place that he called it paradise."

I knew that Adam was the first man. Afterwards there were Abraham, Isaac, Moses and others and they lived in heaven. Everything that happened in the Bible happened in heaven. The Bible was written in heaven and was dropped down to men below. No one ever told me differently. Some of the names of places in Heaven were Bethlehem, Jerusalem and Galilee.

After breakfast I went to swim in the sea with other children. We played little games. There were some rocks where we swam. We had named them after the islands we knew. We pretended to be boats, as we swam from rock to rock.

I was wondering what was beyond the last island. I thought perhaps other islands. If, however, one wanted to go to Sydney, one had to go via Vila and Noumea. If one wanted to go to France one would have to go to Vila, then Noumea, then Sydney, then France. They were all in a straight line. But suppose one took a boat and did not follow this straight line but travelled between Eman and Efate, then one would eventually reach a dead end, total darkness. There one could fall over the edge into blackness, and maybe into the underworld.

In Sydney and France, where the white folks lived, things existed in abundance. There was a gigantic pool of wine, where ships went and filled all the casks they could carry.

Everything existed in gigantic form, and no matter how much would be taken away from it, the form would stay the same. There were the gigantic garden of apples, the gigantic pool of lemonade, the gigantic bag of rice and the gigantic bar of soap, from which small bars could be cut.

We had all reached the last rock, when a call was heard from the shore. It was time to change into our Sunday best and go to service. We would be hearing of the heavenly people again. We would also be hearing that Jesus was stronger than the devil. Last night, however, he had nearly let me be eaten by *Sangalengale.* If he had caught me in my dream, it would have meant that he caught my spirit, and a few days later I would have become sick and died.

As I struggled ashore, I thought that when I grew bigger I would take a boat and explore beyond that last rock to Sydney and France, and see all those gigantic things for myself.

I put on my clothes hastily. I was afraid of getting to church late. I ran almost the whole way, but I slowed down to a walk for the last fifty yards. I was afraid that if I ran all the way to the church door, God would think that I did not respect his church.

Some children and a few men and women were already in the church. There were seats to the left and to the right of the passage that led to the altar. The men sat on the right, the women on the left. Children sat in front, boys to the right, girls to the left. The very little children had the choice of sitting where they liked. They could stay with their mothers or their fathers, or they could sit in front if they wanted to. When I was little I sat with my mother, because her lap was softer than the hard bench and because I could go to sleep on her when I felt tired. But I could not sit there now, because that would be considered unmanly.

The church was full by the time the second bell went. I could hear men clearing their throats, and I wondered why. Were they getting ready to sing, or was it just a habit? Suddenly all of us shot up to our feet as the church elder entered. Someone began to sing a verse from a hymn which everybody took up. At the end of the hymn I watched the elder raise his hands as if to bless the congregation and he said:

"God is a spirit and those who worship him must worship him in spirit and in truth." Then he said a little prayer and after that everybody sat down. He cleared his throat and announced the first hymn of the day.

I hated hymns, because everybody had to stand up to sing them. Some hymns were good, because they were short. But some had many many verses. By the time they got to the last verse of a long hymn, my poor legs could hardly support me. It was considered very wrong to sit down in the middle of a hymn. I had done so once, but my father came and lifted me up on my feet again. I felt very embarrassed. From then on I would make a point of sitting right next to the wall, so that I could lean against it for support during the long hymns. Sometimes, when I had no hymn book, I would count the verses. I could tell the beginning of the next verse, because they would start the tune from the beginning. I would tell myself:

"One verse gone . . . two verses gone . . . three verses gone . . ." There were usually four to a hymn, but a few had five or even six verses. Then I would be caught out, as I sat down at the end of the fourth verse. I wasn't the only one apparently, for since then they have added a long drawn out Aaaaaaaaameeeeen at the end of a hymn, so that all those without a book could know when to slump on to their seat at last.

After the first hymn the elder gave the "Children's address". He began and said:

"Children, some of you have recited the Ten Commandments in your catechism. I wonder whether you have noticed that there is one Commandment that is unique among all the others. It is the only commandment that has a promise or a reward after it. It is the eighth commandment which says that you should 'Honour thy father and thy mother, that thy days may be long upon the land which the Lord thy God giveth thee'. The command is 'honour thy father and thy mother'; the reward is 'that thy days may be long upon the land'." He elaborated on it, repeated himself a few times and that was our address.

Previously we were then allowed to leave the church and we were supposed to wait outside for our parents. But that privilege had been taken away from us, because someone had found out that we weren't simply waiting outside, but were climbing coconuts, were making little gardens and playing games — all activities that were not proper on the Lord's day. From then on we were made to sit through the adults' address, so as to keep us out of mischief.

So I stood through another hymn, heard the reading from the New Testament, then another hymn and the reading from the Old Testament. At last we got to the sermon. I heard the beginning of it which went something like this:

"Everyone has sinned and come short of the glory of God. We are doomed to die in hell, but God loves us and sent Jesus Christ his only son to die in our place. He has suffered for our many sins and we must accept him as saviour and believe that he died for us."

That was all I got from the sermon. My mind soon began to wander. I was sitting with my friend Kaltang in one of the front rows that face inwards towards the altar. One of the little boys sitting next to us had gone to sleep. Little Kalfau leaned towards the right. There was nothing there to lean on, so his body went down and down, then he fell. But suddenly he stopped. He had woken up just in time and didn't quite make the hard floor. He balanced himself for a short while, then repeated the performance to the left. Kaltang and I watched with fascination. He was just like an old man who had drunk too much wine and could not take any more. Kaltang and I began to giggle.

When he went towards the right again, he went rather fast, because sleep had now really overcome him. When he was leaning over at right angles he suddenly stopped for a split second, then went down suddenly and this time made it to the floor. He missed the end of the bench and plunged head first, as if he was making a swallow dive. He lay prostrate on the floor. Kaltang and I just couldn't stop laughing. Our mothers, embarrassed, dragged us outside. Kalfau, from embarrassment or pain, let out a loud wail that drowned the preacher's voice. He had to be carried out too.

Kaltang went home to his house and I went to ours. Then I searched around for breakfast remains. I found a piece of bread and ate it, wondering what my father would say about my disturbing the sermon.

ARTHUR JAWODIMBARI

Spare That Bird

Since I was a small boy I have been obsessed by this note of warning:

"Spare that bird."

It still rings clearly in my ear whenever I see the birds sitting on top of the trees or flying overhead. I even see the image of my father right in front of me with his hand raised.

In my young days I used to go fishing in the lagoon with my father. At times we would come across a flock of seagulls sitting on the sandy bar. I expected my father to kill some of these birds but he avoided hitting any of them. I would run after them with my toy spear. Whenever I came close to one of these young ones he used to say:

"Spare that bird."

I wondered why I was not allowed to kill those birds because other small boys did.

One day I went down to the beach while playing with my friends. Just then a flock of seagulls flew along the seashore parallel with the breaking waves. My friends dashed off after them with bits of wood but I hesitated. Seeing that everyone was gone I began to run after them but before I covered ten yards I heard a familiar voice calling out "ei, come back". At that instant the note of warning rang in my mind automatically. I turned round and walked to where my father was standing. He then asked me if I was going to kill those birds and I merely shook my head. He nodded and asked me to come home with him.

A day after that incident I accompanied my father to a native co-operative store which was about six miles away from my home. As we were walking along the beach we came across a dead seagull. I saw it before my father did and ran up to where the dead bird was and stood motionless staring at it. My father came up and knelt down beside the dead bird and took it in his hands. I asked him if I could take its feathers and stick them in my hair but he shook his head sullenly. He buried the dead bird in the dry sand and we continued on our journey.

I always wondered what was the significance of revering such untamed birds. I asked my grandmother why I was not supposed to kill seagulls and often she replied:

"They are your friends, so don't kill them."

I once asked my father and he said that I was too young to understand anything about the seagulls. The revering of the seagulls remained an unsolved mystery in my small anxious mind.

One stormy night we all went to sleep but my father stayed awake through the night. After midnight my mother woke up and the two of them started talking about the storm. I woke and my father asked me if I wanted anything and I told him that I did not want to sleep at all. He went out to the verandah and looked out to the sea. He then came in and told us that the storm was over and the dawn was near. As I was listening to him I heard a thrilling cry of a bird under the house. I got up and said:

"Father, there must be a chicken under the house."

He asked me to go down and have a look. When I went out the dawn was appearing in the horizon and I saw the white sunrays of the rising sun. I looked under the house and saw a seagull. I crawled on my knees and caught it with my two hands. Just then my father came down from the house and took the bird from me. I asked him if I could keep the bird as a pet but he looked at me and said:

"No, I will get you one of those red parrots so you better let it fly away."

I took it down to the beach in the morning and unwillingly let it go.

One night we sat round the fire listening to my mother telling us the story about our ancestors. She told us how the Girida tribe migrated from Towara which is on the border of

Papua and New Guinea. She told us that the seagulls accompanied our people all along the coast. My father interrupted and said:

"Jawo, before your mother continues with her story I would like to let you know that seagulls and other birds are our totem birds. In fact they are the spirits of our dead ancestors. They will go wherever you go and they will bring you good luck if you revere them."

I wanted to ask some questions but my Mother started her story so I listened unwillingly.

On the next night my father's elder brother brought us some fish. As he was very fond of me he asked me to come along with him. I gladly went to his house which was about two hundred yards away. As soon as we got there my cousins who were much older than I was asked whether I would become a patrol officer, doctor or priest when I grew up. I just grinned shyly because I could not understand what they were getting at. After they put me down I ran over to my uncle and sat on his lap. I then asked him:

"Father, tell me what would happen if I killed seagulls?"

He replied, "My young hornbill, seagulls are revered by our clan because our ancestors' myths imply that they are our totem birds. Two things will be done if you kill a seagull. Firstly myself and your father will kill many pigs and make a big feast to our clan. Secondly the spirits of our ancestors will desert you and you will always strike misfortune in your lifetime."

I was too tired to ask any more questions so I went to sleep on his lap.

When I entered the primary school close to my home I tried to avoid those boys who chased seagulls. However, I found that I had to play around with some kids so I joined them in games. Whenever we came across seagulls I merely watched them chase the seagulls away. I once fought a boy who called me "woman" for not joining them to chase the seagulls.

That evening I accompanied my father to a mission hospital to see my uncle who was very sick. As we entered the ward my uncle gave me a weary smile and then asked me to come near him. I came near to his bed and he held me with his right hand. In tears he said:

"My son, I will not live to see you grow up into manhood but remember never kill those seagulls. Revere them and you will be a prosperous man in your lifetime and you will also live to be a noble old man."

A few days later my uncle died.

Some time after the burial of my uncle I went with my father and mother to our garden. As my parents were getting food crops for the burial feast I went to collect some cucumbers. I looked up when I heard the thrilling call of a couple of seagulls. I asked my father to have a look. When he turned round, his face was moistened and the tears were already rolling down his cheeks. I came to realize that seagulls meant more than I imagined. I felt humble and the note of warning rang in my ear clearly:

"Spare that bird."

I then remembered what my uncle told me and I said to myself:

"Perhaps I am not grown up yet to understand these things."

Several years later I went with my parents to our garden. While we were working two seagulls flew to a dead tree nearby. My father looked up and told us that those birds brought us good news. When we returned home there was a letter waiting for me. I opened it and found that it was from the University of Papua and New Guinea. I passed the letter to my father who read it with his head bowed and nodded. He looked up at me and said firmly; "This is thrilling news," and then he paused for a while and said:

"Spare those birds when you come across them."

Since then the note of warning has lingered in my mind.

SERGEANT BAGITA
(as told to Albert Maori Kiki)

The Execution of Karo

I joined the Royal Papuan Constabulary in 1916. I was then a fresh youth in Port Moresby. I did my first service in Kairuku. Then I was sent back to Port Moresby.

One day a telegram arrived from Ivan Champion, the resident magistrate at Rigo, saying that the bank in Rigo had been broken and the money stolen. The Rigo station policemen looked for it but could not find it. They searched the whole area for two months asking people if they knew someone who had stolen the money. But without result. Then the authorities sent me to Rigo to investigate.

Karo Alaua and two of his friends, Tete and Mape, had stolen the money. Three of them had broken the bank. I found the three of them on Rigo road and handcuffed them. I did not know then that they had stolen the money. Karo refused to be handcuffed. He dragged his hand, "Why you put handcuff on me?"

I said, "No, *Taubada* told me to come and put handcuffs on you." I lied to them. I brought them to Rigo station. Ivan Champion was in the office.

When he saw four of us walking in, he called to me, "Hello Bagita! You fin' im?"

I said, "Yes we found the robbers who stole the bank."

He said, "How you know?"

I said, "We will talk first." I went inside the office.

Karo said, "Bagita is telling lies. We did not steal the bank. He handcuff us for no reason."

I said, "No, you steal it."

But Mr. Champion supported their argument. He said, "Did you find any money?"

I said, "No, I did not find any money. I opened their cases.

29

I only found a tea leaf packet. No money."

Then Ivan Champion said, "There you are. You are in trouble. You found no money; you handcuffed them for nothing."

I said, "No, they stole the money. You looked for them and could not find them. But I found them, these three men."

Champion said, "Bagita, how you know they steal the bank?"

I said, "I know I will find it out later."

He said, "Bagita, like this I will get into trouble."

I told him, "No you won't get any trouble. You will not be jailed, you will not be sacked or fined."

"The way of justice is not like this!"

"I am sure they removed the bank. Keep the handcuffs on them and put leg irons! Do not give them any *kaikai* and water. Do not give them any work until I come back from Hula."

I waited until they put leg irons on those three. I went back to Hula. Karo was very angry with me. The other two men were crying. *Taubada* was very worried.

"How you going? You waiting for the boat?"

"No, I'll walk."

"What about giving you some rations? *Kaikai?*"

"No, You give me one loaf tobacco. You break one case you give me one loaf. I buy *kaikai* with that."

That night I slept at Bonanamo. Next morning I walked to Hula, arrived there at 6 a.m. I called the village policeman to bring Polo, Itama and Vealau. They were Karo's relatives. I told them that I had already taken their relative – Karo – to jail in Rigo. They pretended that they knew nothing about Karo's trouble. I asked them if Karo had given them some money. They denied it. I asked Polo to give me a canoe and take me to Kalo. I paid them with tobacco and walked to Venupupu and arrived there at night. I went up to the village constable's house.

"You are a village constable. Why are you sleeping? There is big trouble at Rigo. Why are you not looking for this trouble? Give me a canoe. I want to go to Wanigera."

He gave me a canoe and a crew of six. We paddled to Wanigera and arrived there at midnight. I woke the village constable and told him to wake his people up. I lined them up and asked them whether some Jula people had bought logs for their canoes recently. They said that they knew that some Hula people had bought canoes from them. They said that Itema spent twenty-four dollars for a canoe, Polo spent thirty dollars for another one and Vealau spent twenty dollars for a third one. I asked them if they still have that money. I told them I wanted to see the numbers on those notes. I tricked them. I don't know how to read and write. They brought the money. I counted it. I told them that those numbers on the money were those of the Rigo bank. They brought some more money. I counted it until the number reached two hundred dollars. I folded the money and tucked the money in my sack bag.

I told them, "If I am wrong you will get your money back from the Arau District Office. If I am proved correct, you don't wait, you must go and get your canoes back from the Hula people."

I got up in the night and walked to Venupupu. The village constable told me to sleep there. I was very excited because I had found the money. I walked to Aroma and told the village constable to take me to Gabagaba by canoe. From Gabagaba I walked to Rigo station.

Mr. Champion was sitting on the verandah of his house. He saw me and called out, "Hello Bagita, you come back?"

"Yes," I replied.

"You find any?"

"Yes, me lucky, me fin' im one hundred pound."

"Whereabouts?"

"Wanigera village."

"How did you discover it?"

"Oh, Hula people went to buy canoe, I bring the money back altogether now."

Taubada held the money and counted it all up. He was very happy.

"All right. You win one shot gun." he said to me. I still keep the shot gun with me. We came to Hanuabada and we had court. The three of them were given life imprisonment. Karo was sent to Daru. The others to Lare Island near Samarai.

This was Karo's second trouble. He had already served a previous prison sentence for murder. Karo joined the police in 1920. He was sent to Buna in the Northern district with another policeman called Bili. They were told to carry the mailbag across the Owen Stanley Ranges to Buna. Karo carried the mailbag all the way up to Naoro then to Kokoda. When they reached Kokoda, Karo told Bili to carry the mail. But Bili told Karo that he was an old policeman and that carrying mail was Karo's job, because he was a young policeman. After a while Karo asked Bili a second time to carry a mail bag, but Bili refused again. Then Karo got very angry and he shot Bili dead.

Karo's first trouble is remembered chiefly in songs.

> *White man sent friend Epe with Malala Halai,*
> *King and Queen sent friend Savola with inland man,*
> *Sent him with Malala Halai,*
> *Sent him with inland man.*
>
> *Frient Epe used European's mouth;*
> *He said 'Bloody fool' as he walked up.*
> *Friend Savola used Motu woman's mouth;*
> *He said 'Ogagami' as he walked up.*
> *Used 'Bloody fool' all the way up.*
> *Malala Halai's feet walked under the Mao tree*
> *With his shadow before him.*
> *Eroe Tati's feet walked under the Aisa tree*
> *With his shadow before him.*
> *Friend Epe's mouth asked Malala Halai to take over the*
>   *mail bag;*
> *Friend Savola Sava's mouth asked Eroe Tati to carry the*
>   *mail bag.*
> *Malala Halai's heart disliked it, he walked up the Koro*

Polosiri mountain first.
The inland man's heart refused, he walked up the cold
mountain first,
Walked up the cold mountain first.
Pepa Karo Alaua — savage and courageous man!
A true policeman!

Friend Epe's hands took rifle of the man of the deep sea
And placed it on his shoulder ready to shoot;
Friend Savola Sava took the rifle of the man of the
horizon
And placed it on his shoulder, ready to shoot,
On his right shoulder ready to shoot.
Placed it ready on his shoulder and shot Malala Halai
On the cold mountain and turned back.
Placed it ready on his shoulder and shot Eroe Tati
In the cold place and walked back on his feet.
Friend Epe's hands held the rifle of the man of the deep
sea,
Shot Malala Halai and excitedly called the name of Oa
Epe;
Friend Savola Sava's hands held the rifle of the man of
the horizon
And shot Eroe Tati and excitedly called the name of
father Savola.

It was because of this previous trouble that Karo was given such a long sentence for breaking the bank in Rigo. Karo stayed in Daru until he played a trick. He pretended to get blind. The doctor at Daru sent him to Moresby. They found he was not getting blind, but from then on he was kept in Koki jail.

Ume Nou from Kairuku was the head warder in that jail. One day Karo asked Ume Nou, whether he had any debts in the store. Ume said he had some debts, but he could not clear them. He said he owed S.T.C. thirty dollars and B.P.'s forty dollars.

"Do you want money?" asked Karo.

"Yes, I want money. But how am I going to get it?"

"I make money come up," Karo told Ume. "I learned some tricks from the Malay people."

Ume believed him, because Karo had taken the bank from Rigo office by playing a trick, even though the bank was heavily guarded. Ume was happy with the prospect of obtaining quick cash.

"Tomorrow you must get pick and shovel. Take an empty case and a sack bag. You go and dig a hole and put the empty case inside. Cover it up with the sack. Then come and tell me."

Ume did as he was told. He dug the hole on the island which was used for European lockup. There were no European prisoners at the time. Ume told Karo that everything was ready. Karo told him to wait until night when all the sanitary line had finished. (In those days Moresby had no septic system and waste matter was removed by prisoners.)

"You must come and wake me up. Take your wife and daughter with you," Karo said. They waited until late at night. Then Ume woke up Karo. Four of them walked together to the island. Karo told Ume's wife and daughter to stay down below. He took Ume up into the building. Ume was completely convinced that he was going to get wealth from Karo. Karo told Ume to lie on the floor. Ume lay on the floor while Karo took a rope and tied Ume's arms to his body. He told Ume not to move. Karo pretended to murmur some sacred words. Ume waited patiently. Karo took Ume's head and placed it in his lap. He murmured sacred words again. He told Ume to close his eyes. Ume obeyed. Suddenly, Karo took out a knife and cut Ume's throat. Ume could not run away because Karo had tied him with ropes. Karo waited until Ume had completely passed away. He went down and took Ume's wife. He told her that her husband was collecting the money. It was heavy. She should go up and help him. He brought her to the kitchen and told her that they were very lucky people. They were going to be very rich. He held her hair and cut her throat. Then he went to Ume's daughter. She asked for her parents. Karo told her that they were trying to take the box out of the hole. It was very heavy, they could not remove the box by themselves. Karo pretended to play with her hair. Then suddenly he cut her throat. Karo went back to the cell. He opened the door of the cell then walked in quietly and slept. He left the key outside the cell.

Next morning the European warder went to Ume's house for the keys to open the cells. He found no one at home. He asked people in the jail if they had seen Ume. Some people said Ume might have gone fishing. Others said he had gone to Pari village to play cards. Mr. Corphy took his jeep and went to Hanuabada and Tatana to look for Ume. He went to Tubusereia and Pari. No one had seen Ume. The police started to look for Ume. They looked for four days. No one thought of looking in the European lockup on the island. On the fifth day Mr. Corphy went to the island and found the dead bodies of Ume and his family. He brought some prisoners across and removed the bodies and buried them.

At that time some Maiva people had come from Kairuku to visit Moresby. They had returned a few days before Ume was murdered. Mr. Corphy flew to Kairuku to arrest those Maiva people. He locked them up at Kairuku, then returned to Port Moresby. At the time I was in Ioribaiva to investigate some shotgun trouble. When I returned some people told me that Ume had been murdered and that Mr. Corphy had gone to Kairuku to arrest some Maiva people.

"Why didn't he wait for me?" I said.

The Governor was looking for me. I was taken to his office and he told me to carry out the investigation. He said; "Bagita, your sleeping places are Manumanu in the west and Gabagaba in the east. You must find the murderers."

I told him I was not going to look for the murderers in those places. I said, "I will stay in my house and look for the murderers."

This worried Mr. Corphy. I started my investigation. Next morning I told Mr. Corphy to take me to Koki jail. He took me in his jeep to Koki. I told him to bring the night sanitary prisoners out. There were forty-four of them. They all lined up. They were in four lines. I inspected all four lines. I paid attention to their eyes. I know if a Papuan has stolen something or has killed somebody the first sign would be the movement of his eyes. When I had completed the round, I asked Mr. Corphy if there were other prisoners inside the prison. He said there was only one man with bad eyes.

"What is his name?" I asked.

"Karo," replied Mr. Corphy. By this time Karo pretended that he was getting blind. He could not walk.

"Shall I bring him out?" asked Mr. Corphy.

"No, I will see him inside." I went inside and saw him sitting down. "Good day, *nakimi*," I said. I called him "brother-in-law" because I was married to a girl from Hula.

"Good day *nakimi*," he replied.

"Good day Karo, how are you?"

"I am all right," he replied. I went and sat near him.

"Karo, can you hear me? If you listen to me, government will look your way, if you tell me lies you will get into big trouble."

He thought for a while then at last he said in a very quiet, apologetic voice, "Yes, *nakimi*, I killed Ume and his family, because Qoava told me."

"All right, leave that there," I said to him. I went and called out to the brothers Corphy, *"Taubada,* George Corphy and Tom Corphy, come inside."

Both of them came inside. George Corphy sat on Karo's right side while Tom Corphy sat on his left.

"Taubada, this Karo he speak Ingilis, he understand Ingilis very well. I found out from him. I found out the trouble. Now you write down what he says. I am not a reporter."

I went outside and rolled my tobacco. When they finished taking all the stories from Karo they came out and told me:

"Oh very good, Bagita, you catchim true."

They told me that this was Karo's third major trouble. First he killed the policeman on the mountain. Then he stole the money in Rigo, then he killed Ume and his family. He must be hanged.

Karo was taken to court. His hands were handcuffed, leg

irons put on his ankles. He was found guilty of killing Ume and his family. He was sentenced to death. He admitted the killing. In Koki he had told me that Qoava had asked him to do it. But in court he said, only himself. The judge told him that his neck would be cut off on Wednesday. Mr Corphy and I took him by his hands. While we were about to leave the steps Karo said:

"*Taubada,* excuse me, I want to talk."

"What talk?" asked Mr. Corphy.

"I want to talk to the judge. I want to tell the judge that Qoava told me to kill Ume. No good, they will cut my neck. I want to tell the judge about Qoava."

We took him back to the judge again. When the judge heard what Karo had told us, he said,

"Why don't you tell me first? You see, I have already closed my book. If you had mentioned Qoava's name, you both would have been hanged together. Now Qoava is going to get a life sentence and you will be hanged alone."

Karo cried. I felt for him. We took him to Koki prison. I scolded him at Koki prison. I told him that it was his own fault. Why didn't he mention Qoava's name? He was sad. He said, "It does not matter. It was my fault, therefore I will die alone."

The day he was hanged, it was a very fine day. Plenty of people came. Many women were crying. Some of them were not his relatives, but it was the first time they had witnessed the white man's capital punishment. We brought him up to the platform, which was already built by the prisoners for the occasion. We tied his hands together, put a belt round his body, then put a rope round his neck, and put something to crush his neck. We stood aside. Then they told him, "Karo, you say goodbye to everybody. Today is the day you die."

Karo called out, "All my friends from Kerema, Koiari, Hanuabada and all other places. Today you are all watching me. I am going today, alone. Do not do like I did. Because of my troubles, today I am going to die alone. That is the end of my talk."

"You finish your talk?" the judge asked.

"Yes," Karo replied.

We put a piece of cloth on his face. All the Europeans who were standing on the platform took their hats off and called to Karo.

"Goodbye Karo."

Then suddenly the lever was lowered. Karo hung like a wild boar. They sent me to see. They told me to watch for any blood.

"If blood comes out of his mouth, nose and ears, you call out." I went and saw the blood coming out. I felt the pulse on his leg. I thought he was dead. I called the doctor.

"Doctor, you come and see him. I think he finish."

The doctor went and felt his pulse and called out that he was dead. They called the prisoners to bring the coffin. They took him off and placed the body in his coffin and took him to Badili Cemetery — where the government store is now. I was very sad on that day. Many people were crying. They were told that they must not do the same thing.

Oh Karo Alaua! Half Kerema and half Hula. Very strong and handsome. A typical Kerema. Feared by many people because of his strong temperament. Envied by many whites. He died in the eyes of his tribesmen, and his mother's people were all there. Papuans saw one of their kind dying at the hands of the white men. This was their law. Papuans must obey it — or they would follow the same track.

This happened in 1936 and the Keremas made many songs about this man: *Pepa Karo Alaua, Epe Savola!*

LEO HANNET

Disillusionment with the Priesthood

When I was five years old, I thought priests were wonderful, because they wore trousers. They looked different from anybody else. They looked white and wealthy and they wore a variety of beautiful garments and everybody paid them special respect. Christianity had a lot of prestige on Nissan Island in those days. If there was a service at the other end of the island, we would all walk over there and attend it. I suppose it was the novelty of being a Christian that excited people. My father was one of the first converts in the village and as far back as I can remember I wanted to become a catechist like my uncle.

But it was not until I was ten years old that I first seriously thought of going into the priesthood. That was the time of our first communion and it made an overwhelming impression on me.

We had been trained for this important event for a year and a half. We had learned the prayers by heart, and the formulas and the rituals. Again and again we had been repeating them word by word. We were told that we would receive Jesus into our body and that we would become new types of people.

Then one day we were made to get up very early. I lined up with about thirty others, proudly wearing the new *laplap* I had forced my parents to buy me for this day. To me this was the greatest day of my life, on which Jesus was going to enter my body.

I felt elated, yet I had difficulty even with this my very first confession. We were supposed to reveal every little thing that we had done. Whether we had hit someone or stolen something; and whether we had played up with some girls.

But in our society there was a lot of boy-girl sex play among the very young.

Boys of fifteen or sixteen would have to exercise restraint but we young ones were merely laughed at when we played around. To our people there is nothing better than *love* and they would not think of blaming small children when they played that sort of game.

I could remember that when I was about five years old, some older children had forced me to act this mother and father game — but now I was too ashamed to tell the priest about it. My mind had already been spoiled by this new ritual and I had been made to think of it in terms of sin. So I had to invent all kinds of little sins which I had never committed but which I confessed to the priest instead.

My real sin worried me for many years, and even in the seminary I kept thinking that I was finally going to tell it to the priest — but I never did.

After this first communion we had to go to communion every day for a whole week and after that we had to make our weekly confession. And still I kept making up sins to give the impression that I was not hiding anything. I repeated the same thing all the time:

"I stole someone's food; I told a lie to my parents; I was lazy at school; I spoke badly of someone else; I talked too much; I didn't say my prayers; I didn't pay attention to what the priest was saying."

Some priests were very hard on us and would make us recite the whole rosary. Others were more lenient and asked us to recite an act of love, which is a formula for inciting you to love someone. This was always followed by an act of contrition: telling God that you were very very sorry for what you had done.

We had to learn all this in English, even though we knew little more English than "father". Much later, I discovered that for more than a year I had repeated, parrot like, the formula I had learned with my first confession:

Bless me father, I have sinned very much this is my first confession . . .

When I finished my primary standard four, I was sent to the Marist Brothers at Kieta. During the first week we were given cards to fill in to say what we wanted to become, when we left school: priests, brothers, catechists, council men, *kiaps* and so on. I chose the priesthood without any hesitation.

Those of us who had chosen the priesthood were immediately given special privileges. The brothers came and talked to us more often. They showed us more kindness. I did well at this school and after doubling standards five and six I was sent on to the preparatory seminary at Chabai on Bougainville Island. Here we were to get used to the idea of priesthood and were to practise obedience.

We had twenty-eight rules to observe: when to wake up, when to keep silent, how never to look a woman in the eye and very many small little rules, so many you could not avoid breaking them. For the first year I was terribly pious, observing everything as best I could, but during the second year I became rather lazy, because we spent so much time working in the garden.

There was a convent near the school, but of course we were never allowed any contact with the girls. We were never allowed to be alone with a woman, not even a close relative, without special permission from the priest. We were taught to keep aloof and that we must speak to women only of things that were holy. We were told never to look a woman in the eye, lest she might tempt us. We were to look past her into space.

Looking back now, I feel that in the priesthood one feels much more tempted by women than outside it. Many priests I knew seemed to look on women not as human beings, but merely as symbols of sex and sin.

But at the time I was not critical of these things. I worked very hard at my Latin in those two years, and my motives for becoming a priest became much purer. They were now based on religious ideas, and I was not merely seeing the priesthood as a status symbol as in my earlier days.

Becoming a priest now meant that I was to be the servant

of no man, but that I would serve Christ who is God. I would be able to deal directly with God, I would hold Him, I would create Him by saying mass, I would use words that would make God come!

At the same time I was filled with some kind of missionary zeal. I must help to free my people from their benighted state of superstition, must save them from the sins in which they had wallowed so long. The European missionaries would leave one day, and we the local priests would have to take over the work. I saw my vocation.

At a certain time of the year we had a retreat. All school was stopped. We had to retreat to think about ourselves and to imitate the Saints. Some of the students took this very seriously and they would castigate themselves. One in particular beat his head with his fists every time his mind wandered during a service and he would use exclamations like "My God help me!" But the rest of us thought him a bit strange.

At birth I had been given Leo as my patron Saint, the Pope who had driven the Huns out of Rome. At confirmation I was given the patron of Saint Joseph, the husband of Mary, who was chaste and who never thought evil of Mary and who was a model of chastity. But I was much more attached to the Saints I had picked myself. The first was Saint Philomena, whose name was found on a stone in the catacombs. The myth says that they tried to force her to marry a man she did not love. But she suffered torture in order to remain pure. I was very dedicated to her, and it came as a deep shock to me later in Rabaul, when I was told that she had been thrown out of the Church! I had always prayed to her and had even written off to Europe to get some more books on her life. She had been my intercessor with God, and now I had to be told that Pope John had ousted all the mythical Saints from the Church and would recognize only the historical ones.

I was left with Saint John Viani the Patron Saint of the hopeless ones and the useless ones. Through him, God could still make use of those whom others considered utterly useless. But he frustrated me often, because I felt he was too high above my reach.

In 1958, after completing two years in Chabai, I was sent to the secondary seminary in Rabaul. I was to spend five years here till matriculation.

It was in Rabaul that my disillusionment with the Church first began. In Rabaul we became more conscious of the enormous difference in the standard of living between priests and pupils. In Buka we had accepted this as a natural order of things: as a privilege towards which one had to rise very slowly. But in Rabaul many of the students felt upset when on a big feast day we had to kill a cow for the priests, and after doing all the work of the cutting up we were merely given the head and some odd bits and pieces, while the priests enjoyed all the good meat. One of the seminarians got so annoyed that he sneaked out a letter to the Bishop of Bougainville about it. Of course, according to the rules of the seminary, all our letters got censored, but this one found its way out and the Bishop was very kind and wrote back asking why they were treating his boys like that? Naturally the Father was very wild with us for giving the seminary a bad name.

But these were minor matters. What really upset me in Rabaul was the discovery that the priests themselves were not free from racial prejudices. At the time there were two cinemas in Rabaul, one for natives and one for Europeans. The Fathers, trying to be liberal, I suppose, occasionally took some of the light-skinned students to the European cinema: the Gilbertese, some Papuans and one or two Tolais. We Solomon Islanders were told that we were too black!

But we did not only have two different cinemas, we also had two different masses: one for Europeans and one for natives.

I remember that once a Papuan came into the European mass, and he was literally chased out of the church by the Australian priest, who, incidentally, was a member of the Legislative Council!

The mission was placed in the middle of a large plantation

and frequently I was sent to do adult education work among the labourers. But I found it very hard to talk to them about the kindness of God, when I saw how badly they were treated and how poorly they were paid. In fact the labourers on the mission plantation were no better off than the workers on the private plantations. They lived in large, rough dormitories and their food was cooked in a forty gallon drum cut in half. In those days they received ten shillings a month in wages. They had to start work very early in the morning and the brother in charge treated them roughly and would even beat them occasionally. I was deeply shocked to find many homosexual practices among the labourers. They were all married men, but the Church, that always talked about the holy unity of the family, forced them to live in dormitories and did not allow them to bring their wives.

When I returned to the mission station from the labour camp it always seemed to me that the Bishop lived like an aristocrat. He kept himself very remote from us and didn't even know the names of his students. Sometimes when he brought important visitors to the school, he had to feign familiarity with us in order to hide the fact that he didn't know our names.

Yet my disillusionment in Rabaul was not really with the Church as such. I still knew that our Bishop in Bougainville was very kind and I simply began to distinguish critically between different missions.

In Rabaul I first became aware of the jealousies between the different Mission societies. The seminary was a regional seminary; it was not supposed to be attached to any mission but it was directly under Rome. It was the Pope's own seminary, yet the different missions were all competing. The Sacred Heart Fathers in Rabaul would always point out to us that by joining their mission we would be better off and have less financial worries than if we became secular priests. The Marists from Bougainville would come from time to time and tell us we must become Marists, because it was always best to go through Mary; and the Holy Ghost Society would tell us that it was better to go through the Holy Spirit because that would bring us nearest to the Holy Trinity.

All this was against the principles of the seminary. They were supposed to teach us about religion in general — not about their particular brand of devotions.

I had always thought of the priests as very very holy men, but now I began to see their jealousies and the competition amongst them.

In 1962, while I was still in Rabaul the famous Hahalis affair blew up. I was emotionally involved in the whole thing, because I had gone to school with Francis Hagai, who was one of the leaders of the Hahalis Welfare Society. At Kieta he had been the prefect in school when I was the youngest student there, and he always looked after me at the time.

The way I saw it, the Hahalis Welfare Soceity was merely out to improve the material lives of the people. The Church had started them off on this road with the foundation of the St. Joseph's Welfare Society, which had collected money to build better homes. The people had been induced to become carpenters in imitation of the husband of Mary.

Thus it was the Church that had made people conscious of the need to better themselves. When the Government came and asked them for taxes, they wondered whether they should give away all that money (for which they would see little return) when they might in fact use it to build themselves better homes. Instead of paying the money to some remote government in Port Moresby the people decided to use it for something that would change their lives substantially.

But the Church took a very different view of Hahalis. From the pulpit they denounced all the Hahalis women as prositutes and they interpreted the whole movement to be nothing but a cargo cult.

I felt that the priests had misunderstood the whole thing. I was deeply disappointed at the way in which they denounced Hahalis in public. It is completely against our custom to put a man to shame in public, because of all the family and in-law ties. I could not bring myself to believe that my people were as bad as the Church had made out. I loved my people too much. I knew that cargo cults existed. My father, like the rest of the people, had been involved in such activities — in spite of the fact that he was a catechist. Like most people of his generation he led a kind of double life. But I felt that the Church had lost touch with the people — that if they had given better leadership, instead of rejecting Hahalis outright, they might have led the people the right way. And so over the Hahalis issue my loyalty was split between my people and the Church.

For the first time also, I became very critical of the Administration; their attempt to solve the whole issue simply by flying in police was extremely insulting.

My awkward position between my people and the Church got highlighted every time I went home on leave. Each time the priests were giving me a little more respect, because I had risen a little higher towards the priesthood. They would give me special presents and invited me to meals at their table, but when I went there with one of my brothers they would ask me in and leave him standing outside. The better they treated me, the more aware I became of how they treated the rest of the people. Eating at their table, I could well remember the days when I was a house-boy in the mission. Often the priests were feasting when a boat with new goods had come in. I would stand there in the background and they would go on talking late into the night and wouldn't care a damn whether I was hungry or not . . .

I was embarrassed, when they told me about the evil ways in which my people were living. They would not hesitate to tell me all about the sins of my own brother — to talk like that was completely taboo in our own society, but they either didn't understand that or they didn't care.

My senior brother, who was a *kukurai* and a catechist, got no such special treatment. When he had to go and see the priests they made a point of keeping him waiting. The church paid him only ten shillings a month and two sticks of tobacco for being a catechist, and the government only gave him occasional token gifts for being a *kukurai*. He became very bitter and once he told me:

"Next time I shall go to the church naked, because clearly that is expected of me. Next time I will go to the government naked! I am forced to stay at home doing the work of the church and the government instead of going to the plantation to get money to improve my family . . ."

The more I saw of the attitudes of the priests in Rabaul and at home the less I wanted to become one. But I was in a real dilemma, because my people trusted me and they thought that I was going to the highest secondary school in the Territory and they expected me to complete the course. So although I was beginning to have grave doubts about my future, I went on to the Higher Seminary in Madang. The decision was a hard one and at times I was even thinking of escaping it all by becoming a monk.

The rector of the Madang Seminary had come to Rabaul and told us about the different life we were going to lead in Madang. We were going to live in separate rooms and we were going to enjoy better food. We were going to be treated like adults and we were going to make our own decisions. However, when we got there, it was dormitories once again and we were treated like children once more and forced to obey all sorts of regulations. The Bishop explained it all away: we had to be modest, we had to practise the virtue of poverty and so on and so on. When we complained about the food we were told that we were too materialistic.

The Madang Seminary did one very important thing for me: the course in philosophy we were given enabled me to make more critical judgments. I became much more aware of the world outside the seminary. In Rabaul I only saw the conflict between the church and the village but now in Madang I was first conscious of wider issues. This was the time when the Bougainville copper issue first came up. It was also the time of Mr. Eastman's U.N. Mission. All these things made us think a great deal about New Guinea as a whole, its political future, and its social problems. I was then much influenced by another student, John Momis, who had received all his secondary education in Australia. Together we formed a group of students to discuss these issues. But the priests disapproved of this: they were always blessing the *status quo*. They blamed Momis and me for the growing restlessness among the students. Finally we called a meeting with the Fathers and the students in order to express some of our views. The priests told us to talk openly and to air all our grievances. We took their word for it and told them exactly what we thought of the attitudes of the priests to New Guineans; how they supported the principle of double standards etc. etc. But the rector of the seminary took offence and he wrote back to the Bishop of Bougainville asking him to remove us from the seminary.

But the strangest part of it all was that though the priests were so critical of John Momis and Ignatius Kilage and myself, yet they used us as show pieces when important visitors came to the seminary. Sometimes they used us to prove that they were providing a liberal and progressive education. When the United Nations Mission came to Madang, Mr. Eastman from Liberia said that we were the only *elite* group in the Territory and the seminary was about the only institution in the whole country that he praised. The priests were most ambivalent about the whole thing.

But we took our cue from Pope John, who was a very liberal Pope and who wanted dialogue with all other religions and all other attitudes to life. So we believed that even as priests we should be open and that there was no subject that we should not discuss.

It was in this spirit that we started the magazine *Dialogue* as a means of communication with other tertiary institutions, like the Papuan Medical College and the Teachers Training College. I was chosen as the editor. The first issue we brought out was a very mild one. Our theme was *brotherhood*. We said that in spite of all the differences in the Territory we were all brothers under the skin. We also talked about the misuse of "freedom" in the world today and we criticized the corruption and the promiscuity of modern society. This went down well with the Administration and with the Church. We got many letters of congratulations from the Church and from people like J. K. Macarthy, Dr. Gunther, Professor

Spate and Mr. Justice Minogue. Even some of the planters wrote in to express their approval. Several sent us money.

The second issue was very different in tone. This was the time of the Tonolei timber lease on Bougainville. The Administration had made the Buin people sell 500,000,000 super feet of standing timber for only $60,000, whereas previously they had paid the same amount of $60,000 for only 200,000,000 to the Vanimo people. This seemed blatantly unjust. Moreover a simple calculation showed that owners had in fact received a mere four shillings and sixpence per acre of good timber! At the same time Conzinc Rio Tinto Australia (C.R.A.) was negotiating for land on Bougainville to mine copper; and again the people felt they were not being given a fair deal. Only Bishop Lemay spoke up for them as usual.

I tried to express our feelings about all these issues in an article called "Now is the Moment of Truth". I said it was time we stopped patting each other on the back. We ought to start speaking honestly to each other. I was warning the indigenous people — to forestall any shock amongst them — that the white men were human after all, that they were not demigods or sacred cows, though they might assume such postures.

I criticized the Administration, who were always playing the role of our "father", but who in reality were selling us out to the C.R.A. and the Bougainville timber company. I pointed out that according to the United Nations Charter the Administration should be protecting the rights of the people.

I went on to accuse the planters, who were playing a divide-and-rule policy in the House of Assembly, forcing our people to agree with them, yet stabbing them in the back.

I said that the Church was always talking about the dignity of man and about the enhancement of the personality — but how could we enhance our personalities when we were left in the mud with no one to support us? When the Church was not living up to her own vows, must we still believe in Christianity? Or was the crucifixion merely a cruci-fiction?

I concluded that the Church, the Administration and the

planters were all birds of a feather.

We printed one thousand copies of this issue and we sent it out to all the District Commissioners, the important people in the Administration, the Bishops and Church people and even to people in Australia.

At the time our rector was away at a conference. One of the priests saw a copy of the magazine and he was very upset. He said he had been unable to sleep that night and that he was disgusted with us. We still had 500 copies left to distribute and he wanted us to burn the lot. He spent a long session with us reading a section from St. James, where Jesus talks about how we ought to be very kind to our fellow men. We reminded him that he had himself been very critical of the Administration only the previous day – and he felt extremely hurt.

We sent out the remaining 500 copies and soon we got letters upon letters of complaint and disgust. Planters abused us, Administration people complained, nuns wrote to say they would pray for us. The Bishop of Aitape – who had sent us money after the first issue – now expressed his disgust. Only Justice Minogue wrote in to support us.

I was called before the District Commissioner and I was shown a telegram from the Department of District Administration in Port Moresby asking whether I was a Communist and whether this issue had been written under any outside influence. Some people blamed the American Negro priest for it all – though the poor man was a completely harmless and inoffensive man who wouldn't hurt a fly.

After this issue of *Dialogue* we fell very low in the eyes of the Church and the Administration and the Public. Even in Rabaul, seminarians received catcalls of "Dialogue! Dialogue!" from Europeans. Several people were sent up to spy on us, to worm their way into our confidence and discover the "outside influences" that had made us produce this issue of the magazine. Needless to say, all future issues of *Dialogue* were censored.

Great pressure was brought upon me to resign from the

seminary. Of course, they could not kick me out, because according to the rules we had to resign voluntarily, just as we had joined of our own free will. After the *Dialogue* incident I decided that I would not return to Madang after my holidays. But my people persuaded me to go back for another year, so I returned and stuck it out until I came to the university in 1966.

However, throughout this last year I was already clear in my mind that the Church was not what I had expected it to be and that the priesthood was not for me. I knew now that I must lead a different life and that I would be able to help my people better outside the Church. While I still respected the priesthood as such, the ideal priest was nowhere to be seen. Moreover, I felt that too many of the church rituals had been over-institutionalized and that these things forced you to do a lot of acting and they did not help you to become a better person. Above all, I felt that the Church was not open and not frank and that they had rejected the dialogue and wanted to continue with their eternal monologue.

My main criticism of the Church was, and still is, their attitude to my people. The very idea of evangelism implies a condemnation of our people — it represents an attitude that does not permit us to be ourselves.

Now — several years after I have left the seminary — I am not sure whether I can still call myself a Christian. Perhaps I am more of a humanist. Of course, certain Christian values still remain with me: a sense of dedication; a feeling of obligation towards my people; the knowledge that my life is not my own. I still believe that there must be cause and effect in creation, that there must be some transcendental being — but whether he is the God of Christian worship, I don't know. I am also convinced that there is still a great need for religion in the world. But I no longer believe that Christianity is the only religion. During my seminary studies I have been much moved by Hinduism and other religions of the East. And thinking back on my very early childhood I gradually begin to see some meaning and purpose in the many traditional rituals and formulas my father taught me.

POETRY

JOHN KASAIPWALOVA

Reluctant Flame

Cold bloodless masks stare me, not for my colour
But for my empty wealth house and passion logic.
I dream to see people, they give me leafless rootless logs
The logs are trimmed, they shine in their trimness
Look how orderedly fat and silent they float this earth
With their guns, their airplanes, their cyclone wheels and their
                                                    bishops
And all this like a snake's shining eye, they fix straight my
                                                    looking
So, quickly I say "this is for me, my food, my soul and my
                                                    spirits
Masta masta give me more, I will pray, I will obey, yes masta
                                                    truly!"

I say aa-aa-aa- sah sah sah- aah yessaah
To the logs captive stares believing this for my good
They have no legs, they slithe greasily like snakes
Their thunderous motion blinds my looking face
I do not see the cold seed making roots in my heart
The seed grows, it spreads inside me and I cannot see it
Watered by the mountain fog that covers the deathly silence
                                                    of the logs
But somewhere in my vein my small blood drop begins to
                                                    volcano cry
For dawn wind to blow away the fog, to make my vision clear
To see these logs truthfully moving
Have no giving roots to intercourse the humus of humanity
No leaves to quiver the living joy in the timeless wind
For their motion is timed and their wind is time.

Yet why, why, why? Why are the wooden faces so real? Why?
I look back and see my vagueness dreaming in the setting
                                                    twilight
I look to the right I see fixed grins and armed teeth
I look to the left I see arming teeth fixing its grins
The faces all pale and wooden coaxing and commanding me
                                                    to laugh
I open my face and laugh like a politician
But this laugh makes night inside me and under its cover
The cold pale seed hatefully grows and spreads

It climbs to my brain I stop feeling and begin to believe
It moulds my face I laugh to the outsider's pricking
It fills my arm veins I drop the bush knife for the pen
It paralyzes my eye-balls to kill their sweeping sight
It captures my soul for the ransom of amen
It clamps my balls and I painfully shout out for a white
                                                    vagina
It crawls over my skin and in shame I moist shirt and trousers
I hate myself and my black lover to forcedly love my hater
The cold seed thrives on my destruction.

YUPELA OL FRENDS NA WANTOKS
YUMI LUKLUK INSAIT NAU LONG YUMI YET!!!

This is the white cradle, this is the white pool
This is the white ocean chasm in which we float steerless and
                                                    captured
Black destination with villages of joyful living seems impossible
Made unreal and distant by the thick white fog
The fog blankets over, it pierces — no black density withstands
                                                    the flood
I tremble in fear, the cold westerly chills my flesh and bones
Memory of past warmth swims in my heart like stones
What is this chill, where is that flame to warm and melt me?

The chill is killing the flame, it is everywhere
Chill you're a bastard, I hate you as a panther hates a
                                        motherfucker
Every turn of my head sees your tentacles strangling innocent
                                        kanakas
You have trampled the whole world over
Here your boot is on our necks, your spear into our intestines
Your history and your size makes me cry violently for air to
                                        breathe

Where is that flame!!! Where has it gone!!!
The acid in my heart kicks me with volcanic tremors
My veins, my arteries, they bulge with swelling resentment
I tremble in frenzy to smash open
To let the acid, the fire and the boulder in my throat
Spew outwards into every direction of havoc cyclone and
                                        thunder!
Yet the chill wraps me paternally
Till the inner vomit and rotten boilings appear
Like gentle swellings of canvas sail pregnant with caressing
                                        breeze
This is the vision that fills my fixed eyes.

I must believe the outward form of this chilling canvas
By this I hide from the distressing truth like the midday sun
                                        hiding its day
The pain of castration and splitting-two falsely fade
When I hazily wink my attention on my form from the
                                        outside eye
And like a masochistic martyr turning to the grace of christ
I accept pain for pleasure and call my vomit my 'good
                                        character'
The white fog and all that it devours
Describes and prescribes me with a three-one criterion
SHIT, VOMIT and PROFIT . . .
                        but, but, but in its greedy ignorance
                        the fog will not see that . . .

John Kasaipwalova

Deep in my core that small blood droplet pulses lonely and
                                                    faint
Each day the weighty cover shrieks arrogantly
Vowing to crush and smother the tiny flame within that pulse
I know the threat, my fear piss is streaming down my legs
I will call my ancestors and all the spirits of my grounds and
                                                    waters
They will throw their magic over my body
I will stop pissing my leg and cup my palms around my
                                                    precious flame
My shoulders will stoop under the chilling weight
My back bone will groan and break its suppleness
But my ancestor companions will not loosen my sinews around
                                                    the flame

Green mountains will boast their size and their foreverness
A passing eye will sing their permanency and solidness
But inside each mountain lies a tiny flame cradled and
                                                    weighted by above
People will live, people will die
But the tiny flame will grow its arms and legs very slowly
Until one day its volcanic pulse will tear the green mountain
                                                    apart
To allow pentup blood flow and congested vomit spit freely
Tiny flame of my pulse, you are silent, you are patient
My hands and my aching body will nurse you against the
                                                    venomous enemy
You will grow, you and I will soon be free to grow our love

Stretch your ear to ground and listen to the distant stirrings
Napalm cannot burn out the flames the guerrillas now open
The green chilly mountain is staggering to burst apart
The tiny flame within its own fence is burning into the icy
                                                    centres
Look how the flame came from the ghettoes
The flame kept down by chain and hunger
Once reluctant now creeps obviously into the pale coldness
Chubby Checker gave Elvis the twisting flame to throw
Ray Charles gave the Beatles the explosive pulse to shake the
                                                    total stiffness

That children tempered by this flame will scorch and burn
                                        their elders
Listen carefully, this is but one arm of the reluctant flame
Burning and melting the icy bloodless body

My flame take your fuel from these brother flames
Let not the oceans drown your linking pipe
You will grow, you will grow, you will grow like a boil on
                                        pale skins
Maybe your vibrant lava will flow to burn anew the world
When Johannesburg and New York is in flames
and the black vomit will fertilize this barren soil
But today your eyes are dimdimed and in your enemy you
                                        see your friend
My lover, my me, we will not follow the cold pale reach for
                                        the moon
Our ancestors and our spirits sleep on this earth
Let the lunatics meet on the lunacy, we will use the soil to
        grow our brotherly flame
Our reluctant dream flame is burning disconnected like a
                                        bush fire
But one day, one day . . . one day . . .

Is this the dream of an unborn child — a madman imprisoned?
No! No! No!
The foetus is already a man; the madman is judgement for his
                                        imprisoners
My body has no time for God and the miracles
My poison is your bitter booting and clapping shut my mouth
The voice that will shoot from my stomach
Will be the death axe to smash the ice of my imprisoners
It will not come from heaven nor from the green mountain
It IS the unseen vibrant rhythm from my pulse deep down
                                        down inside
Crying violently for me to open my eyes and the time.
For to wait a thousand years is to wait too long.
Reluctant flame you have lifted your skirt to my eyes
I come up truly for your wavy rhythms to burn

John Kasaipwalova

But how can you and I make live love
Your flesh and mine shivering to make one soul
To know the burning frenzy of our flesh tremble in unison
As we passionately dig into reality the living shape of love-
                                                body-soul?
Yes how! How? How? How can we live the shaping of this
                                                love
When the cold seed creeps silently in the cover of the fog
To make our love limbs cold and our souls sensualess?
How? How? How? How can a dying soul make love, yes how?
Where is that flame to thaw out my freezing deadness? Where?
I must open my mouth in search of air!
Cry my soul body, cry violently
For your unseen enemy has the poisoned knife to my throat!

Black faces staring mutely by the dusty bus stops
Our envy hateful hearts crying tears to see them speed past in
                                                arrogance
Black shoulder bleeding from the copra bags
Our silent spear strikes inside to see the fortnight scraps
Black angelic voices singing the strange alleluia

Our soul damning itself to feel the memory of sensual dance
                                                and song
Black bodies madly showing off white long stockings shirt and
                                                trousers
Our laugh spirits cries to wear fully the colours we know
Black feet uniformed blue carry the terror of baton and tear
                                                gas
Our eyes hate one another, but somewhere we feel a strand
                                                of *wantok*
Black ears glued to the cheap transistors
Our we yearns to make music instead of feeding senselessly
                                                on noise
Black stooges yessarring whitishly to make paper our destiny
Our revolting will be turned against our selves traitors
Black muffled servants clamouring shamelessly for black cars
                                                stigma
Our aspirations will forever lie lost in the mess of paper status

FUCK OFF, WHITE BASTARDRY, FUCK OFF!
your weighty impotence has
its needle into
me!

Please, my black woman, please do not weep your hate against
us
You were not satisfied, please my love do not cry
See my tears of shame and anger, please my you, do not cry
Impossible for me to say sorry without seeing my lies
Please, my black flame say for me what you see
Lovers with cold arms, legs, hips, skins and souls
Must weep their tight vaginas and slack penises
My black woman please do not cry helplessly
Look at my tears, I know our grave of rotting flesh
Crawling maggots rippling over one another
To suck the slimy fluid of our colding flesh
Please my lover my me do not cry your fear and hate
The thick fog closes our vision, yes
I cannot in honest clarity show us the way out of our grave
But take my hand and let our fingers make one flesh
Though we sink captured, I know a memory, I feel a small
pulse
Inside, inside, where our eyes do not see there is a
Pulse!
Inside, inside, where our minds do not now recognize there is
a living Memory!
A flame alives from its ignition and its fuel.

I go past the Palm Tavern
Wantoks dancing one another to the drums
Big beautiful black shouting bursting open
Roofed by rusty scraps, children laughing, crying and fighting
They hit ukuleles, guitars and tins
Music is
People meeting, laughing at Koki
The wind tickling my hair on the back of passenger truck
My smile to you, we say no words, we know
I offer you one betel nut, they talk for us
Wantok we eat our rice and meat together

John Kasaipwalova

Firm beautiful black hands stoning police thugs
Proud feet kicking off the liar's cargo on high roads
Determined wills pulling out the devil's claims
Voices slapping their faces to tell them "white bastards"
Smashing the glassy window shows of the thief
To give the warn for flame next time

RELUCTANT FLAME OPEN YOUR VOLCANO
TAKE YOUR PULSE AND YOUR FUEL
BURN BURN BURN BURN BURN
LET YOUR FLAMES VIBRATE THEIR DRUMS
BURN BURN BURN BURN BURN
BURN AWAY MY WEIGHTY ICE
BURN INTO MY HEART A DANCING FLAME

KUMALAU TAWALI

The Old Woman's Message

Stick these words in your hair
and take them to Polin and Manuai
my sons:
the ripe fruit falls and returns
to the trunk — its mother.
But my sons, forgetful of me,
are like fruit borne by birds.
I see the sons of other women
returning. What is in their minds?
Let them keep the price of their labour
but their eyes are mine.
I have little breath left
to wait for them.
I am returning to childhood.
My stomach goes to my back
my hands are like broom sticks,
my legs can fit in the sand crab's hole.
I am dry like a carved image
only my head is God's.
Already I sway like a dry falling leaf
I see with my hands —
oh tell Polin and Manuai to hurry
and come to my death feast.

Tuna

Tuna you are mirror of the blue
Tuna you are the pain in my veins
Tuna you are lord.

When I set out to catch you
I am a prisoner of taboos.
"Don't dangle legs over the side of the canoe."
"Don't whistle for merriment."
"Is your thought straight?"
"Is your wife having her first pregnancy?"
"Are you newly married?"
All this awkwardness my duty.

But on the market you are the sun.
You darken the eye of the inland man
when he offers plenty in exchange
without bargain — just to get you.

You are worth the pain in my veins.

Funeral Feast

Powesu you have flown away!
You have untied us two
O Powesu!
I am drifting.

You hands,
the axe hands!
Countless canoes they built,
canoes
that went to touch the west
canoes
that went to touch the east.

Your hands that fished the turtles
the turtles
that filled the ceremonial houses.
Those hands
no others were enough for them.
Those hands, which knew nothing:
the anger of the western sky was nothing to them
the anger of the eastern sky was nothing to them.

Now the hands fly . . .
Where will we go?
Where is our name?
Our canoes are gone
the turtles are gone
the sea is forbidden to us.

Kumalau Tawali

Ambush

Outside the village they lie in ambush.
My child, may your anus not want to excrete
they lie in ambush outside the village.
May your penis not want to urinate
they lie in ambush outside the village.
My child, may you be easy to wake.

The Skull

O skull
a smoked old bone
that's what you really are!

But you are the father of this house
your spirit guards us
we fear you.

When a child of this house is sick
you are the cause
when a child of this house is well
you are the cause

Oh skull
you hang there useless
you hang there powerless

Oh skull
you hang there useful
you hang there powerful

Oh skull
my ancestor
mysterious skull
skull . . .

Faiths

Elijah prayed
and from heaven came fire
to consume logs, stones and all.
Pomu called and tuna
jumped out of the water.

Faith in front of us
faith behind us
power hides from us.

Pomu had faith, tuna came
Elijah had faith, fire came.
What is Faith?
What is faith?

LYNDA THOMAS

Volcano

Our throats are dry and tasteless
our hands are weak and feeble
our bodies are boneless

Wake up sleepers!
They use us like playgrounds
enjoy us like night clubs
handle us like machines
they step on us like dirt
regard us like flowers of the devil.

The master is like a mountain:
the higher it gets, the colder.
But master, we are the rocks beneath
on which you stand. Without us
You are no longer a mountain.
How long shall we carry your weight?

It is hot in your cell
we want to be free
if you don't give way
we'll force our way through you
like a volcano.

JACOB SIMET

The Old Breadfruit Tree

When she was young she was a great friend.
Everybody liked her for her fruits.
She would give you fruit before you could count ten.
But now she is old, bearing not much fruit.
She is no longer a friend.
Hearing she was going to be cut down
she bore a small fruit.

Matupit Volcano

In the morning she awakes like a copra dryer.
She starts to give out her white smoke
and makes the air drier.
Her sulphuric smell fills up the atmosphere;
you think it's horrible
I think it's lovely.

POKWARI KALE

Homecoming

There were greetings from the living
and handshakes from the dead.
Familiar faces all, but remote.
The sounds were strange
the scene not remembered.
Small hills had grown into mountains
and had moved closer together
with grey clouds hanging from their brows.
The devil had been around planting unusual trees
leaving wide valleys, dark and green
clear of all human trace.
A big place for himself to reign?
Was I cut off to put roots in the air
and expected to grow fruit thereon?
All was so quiet, so cold, so vast,
I felt lonely and small, like a wanderer
walking through an ancient, ruined kingdom.

Two Poems

1

If we had grown to face
The morning dews together,
We could show our fathers that after all
Their counsels were not wasted.
When our enemies came, with youthful bodies,
We would have borne the children to safety,
Then taken our arms to the front.

If it had been, we would have shared
The scolding, the praise, the worries together.
Together we would have faced the first arrows
To defend our Lukinya Rocks, our indestructible backers,
Whose changing colours we watched
With misty eyes, under the dawning sun,
When our legs were too thorny to carry us there,
And our hands too small to grasp the protective shields.

But tell me, what is in your mind
That causes me to scratch my head?
Yesterday you looked at me sideways,
And since my return you have denied my due.
Brother, the fault is not mine.
It is the path of the whiteman
That our fathers chose for me;
Yet this has deepened my love for you.

2

I did not cook with good wood
For my land is brown with *kunai*.
I used a *kembo* for wood
But there was nothing to eat.
I called upon the elder; she refused.
I called upon the younger; she refused.

Neither sister would dare taste,
For the roaring gully winds of chilling teeth,
And the dark frowning clouds of my mountain lands,
Threaten those dirty women of the plains.
Let them toil in their plains,
Their fat buttocks sweating.

When my Kepaka clouds fetch me,
The deep wet valleys of giggling streams
Beside the lone mossy ridges and stiff rocks,
With the mumble of smoking falls, are mine.
The whispers of my mountain birds will never leave me.
Never will their sunburned faces see me.

BEDE DUS MAPUN

Sunset

She came across the shimmering sea
like a virgin to meet her groom.
The mighty ocean, shrouded in his glory
was shivering like a dying cockatoo
with an arrow in his heart.
As she sank below the horizon
her last golden rays trailed like a train
across the blue sky.
The swaying palms against the white sand
were bending lower with the southern breeze
casting their long hair this way and that
like *Playboy* models
displaying their nude bodies
before the indifferent eye
of the cameraman.

Bede Dus Mapun

My Land

Look here son, be glad I'm going
I am leaving a treasure behind:
let no stranger take this land from you
in his hands it will be a dunghill.
A woman's virginity goes with her first lover
the first cow drinks from the clean puddle
the first child suckles the shining smooth breast.

So be glad my son, that I am going
I am leaving this treasure for you
as I received it from my fathers.
The world I'm leaving will now be yours.
The trees on this land will shade you by day
and by night you will kindle your fire.
The water on it will wash your feet.

And so I am glad that when he was going
my father left this treasure to me.
I watch the envious son of the stranger
for he cares nothing for me.
And my father waits in the sky
and he sees me quenching my thirst in the river
he sees me resting in the shade of the trees
and at night he watches me kindling my fire.

BENJAMIN EVARA

Mud

Dirty old mud!
But I love it from the bottom of my heart
Mud, dirty mud, filthy mud
mud which is in our blood.

We are made of mud
as was said in the Holy Scriptures.
Where is that filthy mud
that moulded me into a human being?
O mud — I love you.

The blind man can see you with his hands
dirty, slimy mud.
The sky is painted with mud
with muddy ochre.

Milo water on muddy banks you drank
as a child at home.
Mud you've eaten
when walking on four legs.
Yes! Mud, *your* mud!

Benjamin Evara

Forgetting Home

Hey, my friend!
Have you now become a Motu man?
I have just come from your forgotten home.
The trees stand tall and straight
in the Purari delta
and all have grown to the same height!

You look like a Motu man
your hair dyed red with ashes of fire;
it shines like a mirror in the Koki sun.
But your name is a Purari name.
The Gulf water laughs at you:
can you forget your home?

The *nipa* palms cracking in the wind;
The tide returning fast;
Canoes arriving from all corners
waves rising higher with the wind
they beat the empty beach like a husband
who beats his wife for losing her child.
She cries: come home, I know you are alive!

— The town has swallowed me
and beer is sweet to me
like a husband is sweet to his wife.
I am a Motu man — but only for a night.
My home lies undisturbed:
One day I might return.

Now the night is deep
and I cannot find my way:
I have become Moresby's red dust.

BROTHER ALLAIN JARIA

It's Me That's Certain

This is my bed of countless dreams.
I sought my bed when I could see,
I longed for it when I understood myself.
The hazards of my life drive me to my only refuge;
I am scarcely aware it will someday enfold me forever.
I rise intoxicated to counter another round.
Here I am, ready to plunge again into my solace.

The past spent night folded me from this concrete world
and unfolded to me a life-long dream –
"Your bed is your passing shadow.
It is the swimming pool where you
no longer plunge and cool your head.
It is the maggots that swim in thousands to the feast."

I sat on the edge of the bed and blinked at the mirror.
My chest heaved as I fought for breath.
In my eyes was the horror of death.
It is hardly time now to turn the pages of my past memories.
In the deepening gloom, will my hooded eyes open
any second now to judge myself again in the same mirror?

The evil beast in its naked ugliness
turned my warm body into a frozen paleness.
When it was spoken of, I closed my ears with both hands.
My parched lips no longer moved.
My swollen, lifeless tongue no longer spoke
and I closed my eyes to allow the brute to pass.

Brother Allain Jaria

No creature has avoided me, I am certain.
Whether you think of me or not, I come, as sure as my name.
I come stealthily and silently as a night thief.
Entitle me with thousands if you like, I am masked in all.
You find me at the foot of the cliff
you have ridden me of rope and rack
you have invented an electric chair for my comfort.
You find me on high, down below, in your bed.
I tug at you every moment lest you lose me.
By degrees I erode you to nothingness.
My every stride is every life I take.
Passionately, I long to hug you in my chilly arms.

Here vanished into the earth a lifeless body
that battled the war of its own life.
My fragments below six feet will not frame my identity.
Blindfolded I passed the clear fountain and drank muddy water.
Come, dig me out and give me back life!
And I will say to you: "Viva in pace!"

Why do you bother me, black intruder?
I am not born to die.
Unknowingly I have been caught by the snare.
I have swallowed the fruit unaware, have gobbled the hook.
If I could have nibbled at the bait and passed on
if I had known you were at the end of the line
I would have avoided the trap.

With soundless music lilting in my heart I have danced
over golden plains and mountain tops
little knowing I was a prisoner of my desires.
I am utterly helpless when I feel the tug.
My reign over the glories and kingdoms of the sea is in vain.
I am despised in a loveless howling storm.
Here is my life then, a price for the fruit,
Oh rid me of the hook that has buried itself in my bosom.
Then I will tell you I have swallowed a deadly bait.

No one has avoided you, nor ever will I.
Fearlessly I face you and no one else.
This monotonous world is a land of exile.
It is the land of the dead, where no-one
remembers me but you.
I pray, remember at my last hour.
Let me go away from this weary world.
Come brother, my own flesh and blood!
This weeping world moans and groans at me.
An old woman, drained of the energy of her own life
complains against me, as if I am not meant to live.
I am ready, fearless of your thousand names.
At the moment of my last breath, necklace me with your
motto:
"Rest in Peace."

FICTION

RUSSELL SOABA

Natives Under the Sun

I glanced at my watch under the street light at the bus stop. It was half past six. The sun had set half an hour ago. Only a few clouds in the West remained red, but were now slowly fading into the night. It was a night, an ordinary night, like a million nights before.

"Yu go we?" I heard the driver shout as I hopped onto the passenger truck.

"Wardstrip Junction!" I returned.

"O.K. *Wantok*," I heard him shout again. The truck was off. It's a night, an ordinary night, like a million nights before, I kept telling myself, as the wind whistled past my ears. Even now I do not remember what made me repeat over and over again that Friday night: a night, an ordinary night, like a million nights before . . .

The wind whistled faster and faster past my ears as the truck sped on, and I felt as if I were hearing a gentle voice in the wind: It's an ordinary night, same old place, same old people and you are going out as you did many times before . . . and the wind cried:

"What's your name, son?" I jerked.

"Jim Simaz," I answered within myself.

"Where are you going, Jim?"

"To Gordons Estate, to see my cousin and brother."

"Is there anything else you are going for?"

"Is that any of your business?"

"Come on Jim, admit that you are going out for something else, as well."

"How do you know?"

"The world all over suspects it. Come on, son, admit it."

"O.K. I'm going out for something else."

"What?"

"Need you know?"

"Does it have to be a secret all the time? Does it have to boil inside you until it explodes suddenly? Does it?"

"O.K., O.K., would you leave me alone, please? Would you mind your own business, please?"

"No son, I'm not going to leave you alone, if you are ashamed or afraid of telling me what you are really going for."

"Ashamed? Afraid?"

"Yes, ashamed. Son, I feel sorry for your body and soul."

"Why?"

"Because right now you are going out to sin!"

"Oh you mother of   ! Go and jump in the lake will yer? And don't never swim out again!"

"*Olsem wanem, wantok?*" I heard the driver shout, as the truck pulled up at Wardstrip Junction.

"*Nogat, wantok,*" I returned. "*Mi tok, 'stop driver please,' em tasol.*"

"*Oh! Mi tink somting i bagarap na yu sinaut.*"

"*Nogat, wantok.* Thank you." I paid the driver and started walking towards Gordons Estate.

The traffic was rather light, as I walked past the Skyline Drive-in. A car pulled up with screeching brakes just behind me, then swerved to the right, towards the entrance, causing me to call out:

"Watch out where you're going, you silly old colonialist bastard!"

My anger cooled down and I walked the rest of the way thinking of the words of the wind in the passenger truck:

"You are going out to sin."

Yes. I admit that. I am going out to sin. Like I did many times before. Yet how beautiful it is, when it is a secret all the way. Then I remembered a poem, written by my younger brother, Romney Simaz, who ran away from school at fourth form and got a job, because he thought the Mission was indoctrinating him. (He keeps telling me that when the white man first came here we got the land and he had the Bible.

Now it's becoming the other way round.) I began to say the words of the poem within myself, to the rhythm of noise I was making with my footsteps:

Ah! Body!
I heard her cry
once in her lifetime and mine.
It was like rain pouring down
the empty gutters of the naked, virgin earth;
we were lost, gone low down;
then I heard my own voice
and hers just behind me
following me into the dark dark tunnels
of the earth.
I've seen a life
but she, like the rest of shes
hurt me, pierced me, killed me.

People were not flowers to me anymore
they were clad in clothes so fine
and they laughed at me —
she laughed at me also
hated me, snobbed me, killed me.

And I looked up at the sky and saw nothing
looked down at the earth and saw nothing
but people still tell me today
that there is something up in the sky
there is something down in the earth.

To me, sky's sky
earth's earth
all nothings — man's man
and when I hear her cry
and when I see her laugh at me
I only wonder
if she really knows where we were born.

Sometimes I believe her when she says:
Why we were born we shall never know
but I'm sure we were born for why;
but she laughs at me still
when she knows I am different.

She still does not know me!
She brings home her white lovers
even though she knows we went low down
down the naked, virgin earth
and she cried: Ah! body!
And now that she's been robbed from me
all my insides still bleed
when I dream of her cry
Ah! body!

* * *

"Is it you or is it somebody else?"

I was startled when I heard a whisper in Anuki dialect close to my ears. Someone was spying on me, when I was trying to spy through the window of my cousin's house to see if he and Romney were in. I turned round to find a girl standing behind me. She grinned, showing a row of white teeth in her dark face. She certainly was not Kinta, my cousin. She was young, when I looked at her by the light that came from the window, and after looking at her, up and down, for a while, I kept telling myself that she wasn't bad — not bad at all.

"Hello," I said.

"Hello," she returned, still grinning. "Is it you, or is it somebody else?" she asked again in Anuki. She turned her face away slightly, but watched me still with the corner of her eyes waiting, perhaps, for an answer to her question. We have our own way of approaching *wantoks* whom we think we know, or whom we are not sure about. Anuki people always ask this question and either cough or walk away slowly, while waiting for an answer. If there is no answer, then surely the person who had been asked is not Anuki.

"Yes, it's me. And what are you doing here?" I spoke in English.

"My language is not English," she returned in English and looked up to the sky. The moon was full and high. One could imagine how beautiful it would be, if one found oneself alone in the jungle or on the beach on a night like this. The story of Adam and Eve would be full of meaning then.

"Do you speak Anuki then?" I asked, still speaking English.

"That's my language, yes."

"Then speak, and I'll listen to you," I said in Anuki. She giggled.

I looked up to the night sky. The moon lost its glory when compared with the street lights below. How sad, I thought. Somehow I found my arms resting on the shoulders of the girl in front of me. She stopped grinning and moved closer.

"I don't think I know you," I said in Anuki.

"How can we not know each other when we speak the same language?" she asked in Anuki and giggled.

"I don't know. It must have been a long time since I left home. That's why I don't remember seeing you anywhere."

"When did you leave home?" she asked.

"In 1959, when I was nine."

"I left in '60, when I was seven," she said. "My father told me to go to Lae, and my uncle took me there. I am Charles's daughter. You know him?"

"I've heard that name, but I don't know the person."

"He too, did not come home for years, like most Anuki people. Once Anukis go to towns and taste Europeans' dung, they never think about going home again, and they'll die in the towns. That's our sickness, I think."

"Right," I said, and looked at her face. It was a sad face. A native face.

"But it's not our fault," I said in English. "In the fifties we were scattered, disorganized by Europeans, and now what do you see? A lot of bloody Anukis spread all over the place; Lae, Rabaul, Wau, here in Moresby — almost anywhere. Well, as the saying goes: look for your own *wantoks* anywhere in this world, for we are disorganized by Europeans."

I stopped speaking, unwilling to pursue a partial argument like that. I looked at the girl in front of me, I tried to pity her, but my blood pressure began to rise. It's a Friday night, I thought, an ordinary night, like millions before . . .

"I came from Lae yesterday," she said suddenly, sighing in a European fashion which irritated me.

"Yes?"

"Romney told me to come over," she said.

"Romney? Why?"

"We are getting married," she said. I laughed loudly, telling her that she and Romney were too young to get married.

"What about your father? Does he know about this?"

"No, I told him I was coming to spend a few weeks with my uncle, Basil." She giggled again. I knew what that giggle meant. I have known many Anuki girls playing such tricks. Deceiving the old man and letting him pay for her fare too!

"You are too young to be doing this to the old man," I said, concerned.

"Well," she sighed again, "I don't know how you look at things. You are educated. But me, I look at things like a native. I was born a native, I was brought up a native. So Romney and I can get married before we reach the right age."

I felt her moving closer to me. Too close. She was soft all over. Then, not knowing what to do, I cracked the old Anuki joke: "The storm's brewing. I reckon it's going to rain." She giggled and broke free.

"Ei Val! Where are you?" I heard Romney's voice, as the door suddenly opened throwing a streak of light upon us.

"There you are," he said, "Oh, hallo!" he added when he saw me. "Here he is, Ves, it's Jim! Come in, Jim. Kinta — he's here." Romney led us in and Val went straight to the kitchen to dish up food.

Ves just came out of the bathroom with a towel wrapped round his waist.

"Hallo, cousin," he shouted, when he saw me. "Long time no see, ah?" he spoke in English.

"It took you a long time to come down tonight. Why didn't you come last week?"

"O well — it was raining." I said in Anuki. Someone stirred in the bedroom, and then I heard the curtains rustle behind me. It was Kinta, looking sleepy.

"Hallo darling," she said. She likes teasing me.

"Hallo baby. How are you? are you sick, or something, or did your boyfriend belt you up?"

"No," said Romney, "some white creep knocked her down with a motor bike."

"Yeah? Let's see." Kinta let fall the bedsheet with which she'd wrapped herself, showing her left cemented arm, which was hanging in a cloth swing.

"How did this happen?" I asked.

"The bastard was too busy watching his girl friend on the other side of the road. He didn't see Kinta and knocked her over," said Romney. He was angry. I wondered why Romney, my junior brother, looked so wild, rather than handsome for Val's liking. I felt that for the first time in my life I had something really definite to hate. I looked at Kinta again. She was darker than the rest of us, with wavy hair and tanned lips, as if she were wearing lipstick. A Jamaican, she seemed to me. She looked angry and sad.

"Well, don't feel sorry for yourself. Help Val to prepare the dinner," I joked, trying to hide my emotions.

"Hurry up, Ves!" shouted Romney. "It's half past seven." Ves was in the toilet. "Hurry Ves, what are you trying to do? Clean your cock real good? The girls will clean it for you."

"Stop swearing!" snapped Val.

"Did you hear what your own brother just said, honey baby?" Kinta asked me. She winked at me and pointed to Val, who looked at me wildly. It's not my fault, I said within myself, eyeing Val while she wiped the dished. She's not bad; she was brought up in town, ate good food, good everything . . .

Ves came out and jokingly punched Romney on the shoulder. "Ready?" he asked. He turned to me. "We are going to a party at Hohola. You want to come?"

"O.K." I said and rose. "What about the girls?"

"Oh, they'll look after themselves," said Romney. "They won't mind." And we left leaving Kinta and Val to mind the house.

We walked.

At the Skyline Drive-in we came across a few expatriates who had parked their cars outside the entrance and stood talking. A young white woman strayed away from the group, lost in their conversation, laughing too as she talked; and as soon as she saw us approaching she ran back to the group like a frightened white child will run back to its parents on seeing natives.

"You bitch!" cried Romney, aloud in English. "What do you think we are? Savages? Bloody whites! Running away from us, as if we were wild animals." He spat and cursed vigorously.

"Those are the white people, who can't even understand themselves," said my cousin in Anuki. He too spat.

"Shit!" said my brother in English. "They'll go back to their country and talk about living among cannibals even at this age — even in this year 1970! Shit! What do they think we are?" We passed a white man walking alone. We said good night to him and he returned the greeting warmly. God bless him.

We walked on quietly, listening only to the noise of our footsteps and the roaring of passing vehicles. A passenger truck passed us and I heard a University student call out my name in Pig English; "Hey! Imjay! You rascal!" I did not respond and walked on.

"Talk my elder, what's wrong?" It was Romney who put his arm around my neck. Still no response. I was confused. I did not know whether I would get angry with that white bitch who had run away from us, as if we were wild animals. Perhaps I was too emotional, I was not quite sure. Or perhaps I had the right to be angry. These things happened, had happened before and would happen again. White people running away from natives whom they say they are civilizing. Perhaps if I had told my friends at the University they would have told me that my emotions were dominating my reason. But one thing I had for certain that night; I was a human being, like Ves, Romney and the young white woman . . . at a distance we heard a melody on an electric guitar. It was an old and famous song: *Wok abauti long China taun,* and I thought of all those natives who had left their homes just to carry the European's dung and get pissed for nothing.

* * *

I looked at my watch. It was ten to two in the morning. People were still buying beer for forty cents a bottle — which meant that the party would go on for as long as the beer was there. I saw an uncle of ours, a part-time University student, drinking with some Kerema men, who were also students. I saw one of the Keremas tap my uncle on the shoulder saying:

"Mate, when I'm at the Uni I'm a student; when I'm outside I don't give a damn for those fucking whites."

Another student lifted a bottle of beer and said:

"A toast to Papua New Guinea's elimination of colonialist bastards from this country!"

"I'll drink to that!" said our uncle. And they all drank, dropping backwards in their chairs and laughing. No, I said to myself, watching them, I'm not a racist. It's just that I hate the arrogance and stupidity of humanity. That's all.

"My elder, here's two dollars." It was Romney. "Come on, Jim, drink!" And he walked off, swaying from side to side. Poor baby, I thought. Mama would be pleased, if she saw you like this!

Suddenly I thought of Val. Romney was drunk. I couldn't see Ves around. I emptied the bottle I was holding and thrusting the two dollars in my pocket, I came away.

It was a cold and quiet pre-morning, apart from the wild twanging of the guitars, as I came out to the main road. I had not stood long, when a car pulled up in front of me and a white face popped out through the window.

"Hallo," said the white face, "Can I help you?"

"Yes, please — if you don't mind," I returned. "I'm going to Gordons Estate."

"Well then, hop in," he invited me.

"Thanks."

"What's your name," the white man asked, as we drove off.

"Jim."

"Ha! What a coincidence. Mine's Jim too. Pleased to meet you, Jim." I saw him extend his right hand in the faint light, with his left hand firmly on the steering wheel. I took it.

"I presume you were at a party, Jim."

"Your presumption is correct," I returned.

"Nice?"

"Oh yes. A few drinks. Music. That's all."

"Music. Umm. What type?"

"Oh, a local band was playing."

"Oh, not that again! There's one thing I hate most and that's these local bands that go on all bloody night, not giving a damn chance to thóse who want to sleep. Too bloody noisy, don't you reckon?"

Then, instead of telling the colonialist to go to hell, I said; "Yes, I don't blame you, Jim. They really are a damned nuisance."

"My word they are."

We did not speak any more until we got to the Skyline Drive-in.

"You must be pretty brave, Jim?" I asked thinking of the woman who had been frightened of us at that very same spot.

"How do you mean?" returned Jim.

"Well, picking up drunks at two in the morning like this."

"You are not drunk, are you?" he responded a bit nervously.

"Well, I've had too much anyway."

"Well," he said, laughing carelessly, "I suppose it's my good nature: picking up drunken natives on the road. I mean, sometimes they are too drunk and they don't know where they are going." He laughed again. "Once I saw a drunken native lying in the gutter, helpless, waiting for the police, I suppose. Jesus, you could see him! He was the living end! *And* I had to take him home, or he mightn't 've lived long enough to have another bottle of beer. See what I mean?"

"Yes," I croaked in the dark, "you are kind Jim."

"Thanks."

"Could you turn left here and stop, please, Jim?"

"Sure. Do you live here?"

"No. But this is where I am going to spend the last hours of the night. Thank you kindly for the lift, Jim."

"My pleasure," he said. I started walking to the house. "Hey Jim!"

"Yes?" I turned round.

"Are you a University student?"

"Well, yeah, sort of," I returned.

"Sort of? Why didn't ya tell me before you silly old cuckold?"

"You didn't ask me, did you?" I returned, jokingly. I heard Jim laugh in the car. It was a friendly laugh. Then, shaking his head, he said: "It was nice knowing you Jim," then "Seeyah" and he drove off towards Boroko.

I stood for two, three, maybe five minutes before knocking at the door. I was not sure whether I would hate Jim, or like him, or do neither. But somehow, something told me, that in order to to understand people — to really understand human beings one has to get inside them — to find out what they are *really* like.

I knocked. "Kinta, open the door." I heard the light click, the turn of the key and the door was open. Val opened it. She blinked a couple of times before she asked me to come in.

"You are late," she said, "what time is it?"

"Twenty five past two," I answered.

"Where's Romney and Ves?" she asked, and sounded like a mother, who cares for her children.

"Still drinking."

"Ah, you men," scolded Val. "You do nothing but drink! Natives! Always drink too much, not thinking about their wives and children and then they blame Europeans for not giving them enough money to pay for the houses, toilets, electricity and food and . . . " I laughed carelessly, which sounded like a sniff, and I went to see Kinta. I switched on the light and saw her, fast asleep. Sweet baby, she slept like a child who was protecting herself from all the things that might contaminate her life. If Kinta ever did anything wrong — like bring in a boy to sleep with — it would be Ves's responsibility. Ves, being her older brother, was like a father to her. But he is a hard man. And I hoped, as I watched her sleep, that she would not become like Ves. I turned off the light and switched the light on in Ves's and Romney's bedroom. There were two beds. One carefully made, the other unmade — presumably Romney's. I saw a few books on the shelf as my eyes searched the room; there was *Another Country*, a copy of *Cry the Beloved Country* and *Go Tell It on the Mountain*, *The Gab Boys*, *Tell Freedom*, *Native Son* and — half read, lying on the unmade bed — *Soul on Ice*. It was my book. Not a bad collection, I thought, for someone as half educated as Romney. I yawned. I was feeling sleepy.

"Do you want some coffee?" asked Val.

"No," I said. I turned and faced her. She was sitting on a small kerosene drum. Her lips parted, forming a forlorn smile. Perhaps I stared at her too much. "I want you," I said at last, and she understood.

I locked the door, switched off the lights and led Val into Romney's bedroom. While I listened to Val's heavy breathing under me, I thought of Romney, who once in an argument had told me that it was a sin to steal ripe bananas from other people's gardens.

We slept.

WAURU DEGOBA

The Wife Who Came Back

The pigs are squeaking. The children are running up and down with naked bodies, imitating the sound. The newly married women are crying, as their first pigs are being clubbed to death. They are to them their first offspring.

The older women are greeting the visitors. The bright-eyed young woman stands by the doorway, as her first pig is being taken to the slaughter. Her husband, Sopane, the philosopher, the cornerstone, shares her tears too, but he must lift up the pig. He does not want to be disgraced.

The first fire is burning. The smoke rises amongst the trees and disappears in the hills. The women ask their daughters to fetch water for the *mumu*. The cracking of stones and the chopping of wood echo from the hillside.

This was the final day of the big mother dance. The tribe of the Kaigunua were exhausted after long hard labour and a long sing-sing. The men had just completed building the big long houses. The women were busy gathering food for the visitors. Sopane was very busy helping and supervising the men. His wife Sukure was collecting stones with the rest of the women for the *mumu*. Then came the decorating of the *tapa* cloth and placing of the ornaments. The children had already been decorated and the whole village was noisy with beating of drums. The bamboo flutes were blowing in the background, sounding the ancestral tunes of the different family groups.

All the neighbouring tribes were preparing their decorations. They did not need a time to come. They could come at any time — before cock's crow or after. Even before the cicadas came out of their hiding places or after. The women were preparing the dry bamboos and the *pitpit* for the lights. The women must kindle the lights, when a group is dancing. The men must shout and welcome the dancers.

The feast had gone on for months. The food was running out. The time had come to announce the end of the sing-sing and of the final pig killing. The god Akekapa had to be honoured. The moon was moving towards the sun and soon the rains would come. The pigs had grown very fat. Now they were delicious to kill.

But there was one tribe that was not preparing their decorations. The Gomia were planning their revenge. This tribe was two handed, two minded and two eyed. The Kaigunua had recently raided them and the sores were still festering.

The dancing had been going on for days and nights and all the people of the central Vaghi valley were sharing their happiness together. The women and the girls had gone to the dancers they most admired. Now it was time for the wise men to make decisions.

"When you fetch your water, you must bring it to me to be blessed," said Sopane.

The water was their ancestral magic. Each family had a secret place where they fetched water when they wanted to kill pigs. If they did not do so, their ancestors would turn away from them, so that there would not be enough meat for all.

During the night, Sopane, Gene and Maima called a meeting. They advised the people how to share their pigs among the visitors. One full string bag of *kaukau* to the visitors meant one whole pig to the visitors. The pigs were brought to the village with the ritual bamboo water containers. The pigs were tied to poles and the bamboos were hidden for the night. The sweet music of the bamboo flutes was blowing through the dust-mist night. The newly married couples were weeping for their pigs. They were crying and singing their chants about the days before their marriage. In the men's house they were arguing and discussing about the pigs. In the girls' house the girls and boys were having a "carry-leg" feast. The girls' legs lay on top of the boys' legs and they held each other and sang their love songs.

In the eastern horizon the orange-yellow tinge appeared. The men were praying to the father. Then the women prayed for the blessing they needed to raise new pigs. Then Sopane made the announcement to bring all pigs to the clearing.

The pigs were squealing as the clubs landed on their foreheads. The early dogs were licking the red fluid. The fowls flew into the bush, as the pigs squealed louder. The children were imitating the noise, to tease the suffering creatures.

Now there were rows and rows of silent, sleeping pigs. The men and women stood at the head of the long lines. The visitors were standing far off, waiting to be mentioned. Sopane took his place in the centre, as the sun heated the earth. He called to his creator:

Arekapa! emina ne yo'.
Ake Kiape kinoyo!

Father come close to our day.
Help us and bless our gifts!

The visitors received their pigs. Blood was everywhere. The women were singing in the creeks and rivers as they cleaned the intestines. Smoke was covering all Kaigunua land. The blood dried up and the smell was peaking. The golden-blue friend, the fly, flew about seeking his share and more.

Sopane's wife was having a *mumu* right in the midst of the women's houses.

Meanwhile the Gomia tribe was waiting. At the village perimeter they waited for the sun to hide himself and for the cicadas to sound their warnings, before they would enter the village.

The western sun had melted and dried up the blood. An atmosphere of rotting flesh hung over the village. The meat was stored away in long shelters and the people were having their evening worship. The dogs lay quiet, digesting the blood they'd drunk. The nightfall was sudden, but still the

yellow-purple clay-like sky lingered in the west. At this time
of day the men must step out of their huts, for Kiau Kumo
Kakai Land — the place of the dead — lay just behind the
next green. Night fell when the sun had reached Nedik
Nediken — the "head of the lake".

Sopane, the cornerstone of the tribe, called out to Sukure,
his beloved wife, to bring him his food. He had not eaten all
day for he had been organizing the activities. Sukure stepped
out of her hut with a bag of *kaukau* and approached the
men's line of huts. She didn't notice the dark figures in the
background as she handed over her string bag of *kaukau* at
the men's house. The older men praised her. Smiling gently,
she hummed the melody of her husband's whistle.

Suddenly she was amongst the people of Gomia. She
couldn't shout, because her mouth was closed by hands. Her
covering was gone and she was carried away, while the Gomia
people rushed into the house.

And the houses are on fire. The lights are shining brightly
so the enemies can see the places of concealment. It is too
late for the men of the village to look for their fighting
weapons. Screaming, the women run into the darkness with
their children. The houses and the cooked meat are on fire.
Some are eaten, some fed to the dogs, some fed to fire and
mud. The Gomias run through the village raiding and
murdering.

It was finished. The village people were scattered. Sopane
had a spear sticking in his hip, but it was just like a scratch to
him. He wanted his wife, Sukure. He could not see her. He
called her name. He shouted her name, running from house
to house. He picked up a big stick and pushed it into the
burning fire. He could not see her. On the opposite peak he
could hear the Gomia people celebrating their victory with
their war cries and their hymnal praises of their war gods.
Then they moved on, back to their home land with the
captured women and girls.

Sopane's people were red of face. The meat was blooded
from the wounds of the dying. Their gods would not allow
them to eat the defiled food now. Tears ran down every face.

Only the little children moved about. Their fingers were on the meat. They ate a piece here and there, unaware of what they were doing. The fires burnt out and the Kaigunua people were left with the darkness of the black silent night.

The murdered ones, the dead ones, the speared ones: all were sent away to the noman's land. The visitors were sadly sent away to their villages. The tribe was in the mood for revenge, thinking of their payback. But Sopane sat thinking of his beloved wife. He could see her face. He could see her hands on top of his, in the dark. He could feel her body, smooth and warm approaching to touch him. He said to himself: I am a man of magic and a fighter. I will prove to my people that I have power over all.

At the first dawn, he set out into the scrub. He caught a little bird. He collected some bush leaves. He made himself a hook. He collected some black ashes to paint on his chest. The sun climbed up to his forehead slowly. He set out with a bamboo of sacred water, some bananas and some *kaukau*. He reached Mani. It was the place of the dead of the tribe. Sopane stopped. He laid everything down on the peak. He got a piece of magic bamboo and rubbed it against dry wood. The bamboo started burning. He put all the dry wood and the leaves he had collected on the fire. He speared the little bird on to the hook that he had made. He stuck the hook in the ground and tilted it until the small victim was right over the fire. He put more leaves on the fire and a cloud of very thick black smoke began to rise. He started singing his magic song, the song of sadness and sorrow. Tears dropped down his face.

Na gee we hei hei
Na kumo we hei hei
Na gee we hei hei
N'kumo we hei hei

Apo Sukure ina yo
Apo Sukure ina yo
Apo Sukure ina yo
Apo Sukure ina yo

Mana kaa-kai yo yo-o
Mana kaa-kai yo yo-o
Na moi to ewe yo-o
Na moi to ewe yo-o

I am a true man of magic, oh oh
I am a true father of witches, oh oh
I am a true man of magic, oh oh
I am a true father of witches oh oh

Father sun, bring my wife back to me
Father sun, bring my wife back to me
Father sun, bring my wife back to me
Father sun, bring my wife back to me

Mother spirit bring my wife back to me
Mother spirit bring my wife back to me
I am waiting here for her
I am waiting here for her

Sopane knew that if the little bird over the fire would burn and drop into the fire, his wife would never return to him. But if it did not burn, then his songs would be blown to her ears and she would notice the black smoke that was rising on the blue mountain. Sopane put more leaves on the fire. He was patient and stayed to finish his work.

Back in the village, the people could see the smoke rising into the air. They could hear the faded melody echoing in the dead man's valley. They knew it was Sopane and they waited.

Sukure had been waiting for a sign in the distant village. She saw the dark thick cloud rising up on the summit, then dying out in the darkness of the mountains behind. She knew it was Sopane. She could hear her husband's voice, singing and calling her to go home.

Ambai barel mongo nono dupere do-o
Nono dupere do-o
Ambai barel mongo nono dupere do-o

Ende unbe mamuno koro dupere do-o
Nono dum pere do-o

Kai meve o-o
Nivi tawa ige-o
Wan marelga o
Kai marelga o was moigo o

Su su sa o-o
Su sa sa o-o

She could imagine him smiling at her. She wiped the tears from her eyes and looked up again . . .

She found herself amongst the rocks and the bush. She kept turning back, to see if anybody would follow her. She stopped at a couple of places and watered her face. She knew now that she was near the boundary. Soon she would be safe in her own territory and she walked very cautiously with her mouth wide open. Then she headed for Mani, where she could see the smoke rising into the air.

On the summit, Sopane was still waiting with his weapons nearby. He was eating the wasted bananas and *kaukau*. Suddenly, he saw his beloved wife close to him. Without a word, he grasped her in his arms, as the sun gave them the blessing. His magic had worked and gave him pride in his fatherhood of the tribe. He turned back to the village, and together they returned.

As the day withdrew, the biggest pig was blooded and cooked. It was his celebration for the return of the beloved woman. Truly he was a great man of magic. Truly he was the cornerstone of the tribe. He was the centre post and the oldest sugar cane. He was the Man.

LAZARUS HWEKMARIN

Man on the Moon

After Jnowa and I had suggested one morning that we must go to the next village and hire a truck in which to drive to Wewak, and then to Brandi High School, which was to begin school the following day, we took a walk down the track that led to the village.

The village belonged to Kuminja, the son of Nama, the heroic battle leader of the Wamanduan clan, who had died many years ago. Kuminja retains some of these characteristics and is still the clan chief. He is also among the higher respected and prominent persons in the whole village. Besides this, he is rich. He has several trucks, a trade store and thousands of coffee trees. He, however, has never been to school, for during his youth there was no such thing. Assisted by his sons and relatives who have been to school, he runs a very profitable business.

We were now halfway towards the village, which was about a mile long. Then we saw Kuminja who came running around the corner, very exhausted. We wondered where he was hurrying to. He pulled up beside us, while still in the mood of running.

"Where are you kids going?" he asked, in very threatening manner. "Do you know that every member of the Womanduan clan, when he goes to sleep tonight, will never wake up, but sleep for ever?"

Being non-Wamanduans, we weren't worried by his words. But we asked why this was going to be so, and he said:

"Because man has landed on the moon, and has discovered the secrets by which the moon controls Nambiana, our ancestor who tells us when to wake up when we sleep at night. So now I'm going to Hunan to hear what Nambiana

102

has to say about it."

Yes, he had heard the news that man had landed on the moon. The moon, as the story goes, is the sexual part of Kwial. the wife of Raman whose descendants are the Wamanduans. One day while out in the bush gathering food, Kwial was raped and killed by men of the Hufan clan. They distributed the flesh among themselves. To an old man they gave the vaginal part of the body. He took it home hoping to make a feast out of it. The following day, returning home with a bag full of *taro*, he found to his surprise that the house was lit up with bright light, shining from the sexual organ. Kwial's spirit in the form of a cassowary appeared to Raman in a dream and told him that she would go to live in the sky and watch upon the clan; that she would appoint Nambiana to be her representative on earth and whose commands must always be obeyed the next day. The next day, the shining lady asked the old man to place it on the roof of his house. The sky came down close to it and the vagina became stuck to the sky. It has since been known as the moon.

Kuminja did get to Hunan, the sacred dwelling place of Nambiana, which is a deep dark pool of water underneath a thick jungle of tall trees. Nambiana dwelled under the water in the form of a large python. An unusual thing happened when he arrived. Usually when Kuminja (who was the only one allowed to go there) arrived at the place, the python would raise its head above the water, and poke out its tongue, while the vegetation around the edge of the pool would sway vigorously as if there were a big wind. But this time none of these things took place. This was a great terror to Kuminja who did nothing but run back to the village. He called all the clan members together and told them of the great disaster that was to come upon them. It became obvious now that all the people had to listen to every word that Kuminja spoke, and do whatever he told them.

Of course it was the white men, the Americans, that had sent the men to the moon. It was them also who had made all the trucks, the clothes, the knives and other European goods that the clan possessed, as well as those in his store. One way to secure themselves, thought Kuminja, was to destroy all European-made goods. He ordered that not a single item of European goods was to be left and seen in all the households of the clan. Every single item must be got rid of and out of sight before anyone could go to sleep that night. Everyone became very busy that afternoon, burning many things that could be burnt. Everyone wore traditional clothes. All shirts, dresses, etc. were burnt, and trucks pulled to pieces and thrown into the river. The store and the office got burnt down with all the equipment and stock. By the time anyone could go to sleep, the scene had flashed into a Wamanduan four hundred years ago. Everything turned traditional.

Everyone wondered about the real effectiveness of this, when they found they were able to wake up the next morning. Whether this was due to the destruction of their property or not is a big question. However, the District Officer had heard of what had happened. He went to the village, made an investigation, and Kuminja was sent to jail leaving the people in despair and wonder.

JOHN WAIKO

The Old Man in the Balus

I looked up again and then I saw the *balus* coming like a bird out of the trees. At first it looked like the smallest *suriri* bird, but it became bigger and bigger. Soon it looked like a hawk. It circled twice, then it came down like a hawk to the ground. But hawks dive to the ground silently. The *balus* came with a great noise. It was like the noise of all the cockatoos put together plus *dunana,* the thunder.

The *balus* came to where I was standing, turned round and stopped. The noise died down. A door was opened and people came out and bags of rice and cases of meat were unloaded. The *balus* looked exactly like a hawk. It had two wings and two legs. It had a tail and a head. But the *balus* had no beak and no eyes, no mouth and no claws. There was a white man who had brought the *balus.* He looked tired and angry and he shouted: *'Ani pasinja?'* Then Yavita stepped forward and said: 'Yes two,' and gave him our *tikes.* We went into the balus and I sat on a *seia.* The white man turned round and faced the head of the *balus.* He touched a small stick in front of him and the *balus* started to shout. Yavita put the *berete* round my waist. The noise was becoming louder and the *balus* began to move. The white man looked back at us quickly, then he turned round again. His hands moved and touched the small black and white sticks and the *balus* began to run like lightning on the ground. Then it dived away.

I did not want to see it diving, so I shut my eyes and bowed down. The noise was very frightening now and all my intestines, heart and everything inside me climbed up into my neck and waited there.

The *balus* rose quickly and Yavita said we were over the

trees. But I still shut my eyes. The noise made by the *balus* now resembled the shrieking of cockatoos when they bite a lizard on a *simani* tree. Yavita did not seem to worry. I knew that he wanted me to open my eyes and see things. But worries came to me like waves breaking on a rock. I kept myself strong, by forcing the words of the evangelist into my skull:

"Our fears for today, our worries about tomorrow: wherever we are, high above the sky or in the depth of the ocean — nothing will ever be able to separate us from the love of God that is in *Iesu Keriso.*"

The *balus* was like a madman who is shaking his arms and legs. My heart did not come down from where it stayed hanging in my throat. The more the *balus* climbed, the nearer my heart came to my mouth. Then for a moment, the *balus* acted as if it was falling like a leaf to the ground. And my stomach walked up to join my heart in the mouth.

When the *balus* was tired of climbing, it put its head straight. Now it felt like floating down the Gira river in a canoe, when the waves throw you up and down.

"I want you to see what it is like up in the sky," Yavita said.

I opened my eyes for the first time. First I looked to see if Yavita was there with me. Then I looked to the left and saw what Yavita wanted me to see. I did not know what to say. The tall trees I see walking on the ground, were not there. Everything looked very flat, like a river. But on the right there was a great fence of mountains that closed in the river of land. The sun was about to sink behind that mountain fence.

I wondered how long the *balus* would take to get to Popondota. It had once taken me a week to walk to Higa Furu, which is near Popondota.

"Will we travel like this days and nights till we reach Popondota?" I asked Yavita. "And when is the *balus* falling to the ground for us to get out?"

But Yavita said, "No, it won't be long before we go down to the ground."

And I was amazed at the speed with which this *balus* could run. I saw a black and white cloud in front of the *balus*. I always thought that clouds were tied to the sky above by some strings. But now this cloud was just floating in the sky, no strings. I thought the man would take the *balus* away from the cloud, but he made the *balus* go straight through it. I closed my eyes quickly and the next minute the *balus* was shaking like a madman. It went up and down like a canoe paddling against the waves in the sea. I thought that the cloud was something hard that would tear the *balus* to pieces. But we soon came out of it and I opened my eyes again.

The *balus* lowered itself and began to circle the village of Popondota. It was the biggest village I ever saw. The roofs of the houses were shining white. On the roads below strange pigs in different colours were running up and down. I was looking down at the white roofs which became bigger. Then the *balus* bent over to one side — all my fear came back to me and then we swooped down like a hawk trying to catch a rat.

The *balus* touched the grass. It ran madly, but the man touched the little black sticks in front of him and it stopped. Then, and only then, my heart and my stomach came down from the neck to their proper places and I took a deep breath.

When the door was opened and we came to the ground, I cast my eyes here and there. I saw a white pig that came running towards us in the distance. But this strange pig had no legs. Its head was blunt, there was no nose, no tail. It ran very fast, as if to attack a man. It came with a noise, like a *balus*. "It must be a wild one," I thought, and I looked around for a tree to climb if it should attack me. But there was no tree near and I decided to hide in the *balus* in case of danger. As the pig came near I could see its two white eyes, but I could not see the mouth.

But to my greatest surprise, there was a man inside the head of this pig-like thing. I was frightened, but Yavita came and said:

"Father, that is a *taraka*. The place for the *balus* is far away, so the *taraka* is coming to take us to the village."

I bit my finger. As it came nearer to us, it stopped running and began to walk and then it stopped. The man came out of the head. I was anxious now to have a look at it and we walked over and touched it.

It was exactly like a pig, but it had no hair, no mouth, no flesh and in fact it had no intestines. I bit my finger again, because there was no string attached to it. Who had made the pig *taraka* and how, I could not tell.

Then some thought suddenly entered my skull and into my brain. I had forgotten to say thank you to God, because he had taken the *balus* safely through the clouds and down again to the ground. When the *balus* stopped and I came down to the ground, I was busy looking at the pig *taraka* and I forgot to say thank you. Up in the air, when my heart rose to my mouth, I was a frightened baby in the hands of God. But once safe on the ground, I felt like a grown man and the hands of God seemed remote. Up in the clouds, there was only God to ask for help, but here on the ground I felt safe, because my dead father and mother were near me.

MEAKORO OPA

He Took the Broom from Me

It was a dull morning when I got up from my bed. It had rained the whole night. Outside I could just hear the drizzling of the rain.

Because of the dullness of the weather time moved unexpectedly fast. So it was 7.30 a.m. and I had only half an hour to get to the office, which was some five miles away in the centre of the town.

I washed my face and put on some rough clothes and got a bus to work. Arriving at the office I found that I was the only one late that day. As I walked in all eyes were directed towards me. There were black eyes, blue eyes and brown eyes. At this, I faced the floor on my way to get the brooms out and start sweeping water out. The water had slipped in through the louvres last night during the rains.

Most of our office folks were angry with me because they had to dry their tables and chairs themselves, which they thought was a job only for me and therefore below their standards.

Though they did not actually show this in their actions I sensed it all the way along. That day in the office was a hard one for me. I worked hard for fear that I might lose my job as a cleaner.

It was lunch time now, and I heard the O.I.C. of the Staff Section say loudly:

"O.K. boys, it's lunch time!" However I did not stop till five minutes later. There was no one in the office now. I left for the esplanade.

When I stepped out of the office, I found that there wasn't anyone around. It was raining very fiercely. The wind was making about seventy to eighty miles an hour.

A short while later a workmate came and asked:

"*Aei,* Lupa, would you like to have some lunch? Look I have a packet of fish and chips I can't finish."

Though I wanted very much to have some, my mind was in the world of serious thoughts. So I nodded rejecting his offer.

The workmate had gone now and I was alone. I thought of all the years of my life. This was the first time I had refused, objected to or rejected any gift or request. For all these years I have been accepting friendly dog-pattings on my back. Now I objected to it.

Unexpectedly the lunch-hour break ended and I saw the office folks rush back from the nearby shops beside the esplanade. Because I had no instrument to tell me time, I started to walk, too. I did not care about getting wet.

We were now in the office and one of the senior native clerks approached me:

"Lupa, come here just for a while will you please?" I walked towards him. There I found that all tables and chairs in his section were in a sea of rain water.

He did not tell me anything but I sensed that he wanted me to sweep the water out. Like a good humble servant I started at the top of my strength to get all the water out and dry the place up so that the clerks could get to work.

Some fifteen or so minutes later I was just about to finish the work I had been assigned to do. I stopped to take my break.

At that moment a young Australian clerk, whom I suspected of being the most racist of all the white people I have ever known, walked across, came to me from the opposite end of the office room and eyed very hard at me.

I could not believe my eyes. I was sort of hypnotised. He spat me in the face and I faintly heard him say:

"You bloody coon", and he took the broom from me.

After five minutes had passed, I was present in my mind. I went over to his end of the office to get the broom back to finish my work. When I reached him he gave me the broom and ordered me to sweep the small area of water about two feet in diameter under his table.

It was over. I went to finish my previous work at the native clerk's section. As I worked away, I tried to rationalize the previous incidents that had just passed.

He took the broom from me. Is he more important than me or the other natives? On the question of importance and priority the senior native workers thought he was *right*.

He was from the *masta* race. He was the "masta". He took the broom from me. A *masta* should be served first. But I wanted to be *masta*, too. He would not allow me take the broom from him.

Yes, it was a hard day. A bad day for me! It was the first time a cyclone was known in our town. Many people were killed. Many houses were destroyed. It was also the first time I had refused to accept friendly dog-pattings.

But despite all these, the most striking thing that went on down deep in mind was that "he took the broom from me".

Would I take the broom from him in some unknown future? When will it be? If I have the chance what shall I do?

Shall I kill him? Shall I do the same to him or what?

I shall kill him. Yes I shall kill his people. I shall kill to possess and take the broom from him as he took it from me in the past.

DRAMA

JOHN KASAIPWALOVA

Rooster in the Confessional

A QUICK GLIMPSE

Gone are the white missionary Sundays. Today we are blessed with our own *Mesinari* (pastors), *Toguguya* (preachers), *Toligalega* (special disciples) and the fine upstanding core of *Tobalesia* (devoted Christians).

Week by week, month by month the village focus on Sundays is usually found around the village church and the *Mesinari*. One cannot escape the feeling that there is a new way of life in the air — there is the smell of civilization at long last.

Women dress themselves in full modesty and practising Christians mark themselves out by wearing long-sleeved white shirts, with white *lap laps* and dazzling black belts girded solemnly around the waists.

The village meets around the church and it is here that the roughness of the week's conflicts is smoothed and settled. Sometimes too, the roughness for the next week is generated here. Saturday and Sunday are The Days.

CHARACTERS

MOSES TOBUDI	Apprentice preacher
MWAKENA and TOPOLU	Sons of Moses (twelve and ten years respectively)
SALOME NAMWANA	Wife of Moses
PAULO	*Mesinari* (pastor of the village)
NOAH KIMAPU	Third Cousin of Moses

CHURCH WARDEN, VILLAGERS, *TOBALESIA*, *TOLIGALEGA*, *TOGUGUYA*, *NAKALESIA* and CHILDREN.

115

SCENE 1

Saturday late afternoon. MOSES and his family sit on the verandah of their house. MOSES is brooding angrily; as he draws the limestick from the pot he bangs it loudly to make sure that the occupants of the next house know his anger. SALOME is timidly throwing the scraps of food to their dogs and chickens below.

MWAKENA *(to Moses)*: I want some betel nut!

TOPOLU: I want some too! I asked first. You are always beating the lime pot and never give us some quickly. You give your betel nuts easily to other men, but when we ask you, you turn your head.

MWAKENA: Yes, some of these men are useless about the village. My small mother told me and . . . *(stops quickly and moves backward slightly as the father glares suddenly at the two boys.)*

MOSES *(explodes)*: What! How many times must I tell you! Your ears are filled with rocks. *(He points to the broom lying near the mother.)* You see that? Next time, THAT. *(looks away from the children and stares into the distance. He tries to give an air of composure again.)* You are school children now – NOT just village children, yet you still have your mother's bad manners. When will the teacher make you educated?

SALOME: Ahh! You are their father. There is nothing wrong with children pestering their fathers for betel nuts. If you don't give it to them, who will? It shames me to see you keeping the betel nuts from the children. Their uncles are still alive and have plenty of betel nut trees. *(She moves for the big basket next to the father.)*

MOSES: You stay away from that basket. So eh, you are going to encourage these children to break the school rules. The teacher has already warned the children at school and on Sundays before the village elders that betel nuts are bad for children's brains. If they chew betel nuts their brains will be drunk and they will not be able to learn anything.

SALOME: How can betel nut chewing spoil the children's brains? I have never gone to school but I know that whenever I chew betel nuts I feel good and my brain works very well. Betel nuts don't spoil the brain. Anyway, I think the teacher is a liar. The children say that he smokes and chews betel nuts in the school house. Only two days ago he sent Topolu to come and ask for betel nuts from me as part of his homework. *(pronounced as "kom wok")*

TOPOLU: Mother is right, the teacher is a liar. He beats me when I go to sleep in school. Yesterday he hit me over the head with the big Bible because I was laughing at his stories about Moses and his talk with God.

MOSES: Serves you right. Nobody laughs about the Bible, it is a holy book. How can you learn if the teacher does not beat you up? Look, I passed Standard one, Standard two and nearly topped the class once, only because the teacher used to beat me every second day. The teacher must beat you up for your own good. I failed Standard three, because I was getting too big and the teacher stopped beating me up, and also my brain was getting drunk because I started chewing betel nuts before school. When I chewed betel nuts frequently, *(he points to his skull)* this thing here started thinking more about women than my tables and the Bible stories.

SALOME: Oh Moses, stop this nonsense and treat your children kindly! Why should your anger about other things fall on your innocent children? Look at yourself. All day you have been sitting there brooding over Jeremiah's Horse. How do you know that he has been stolen?

MOSES: Yes, I know he has been stolen. Stupid woman, don't you think I have two eyes? For two days I haven't see Horse come and eat the scraps with the other chickens in front of our house. *(points to his fingers)* One, two days now!

SALOME: Maybe he has found some attractive hens on the other end of the village. It is natural for roosters to do these things, especially if Jeremiah's Horse is tired of our own hens.

MOSES *(in disgust):* Never, never, never! Jeremiah's Horse is a good rooster. For two years we have treated him like our child. Everybody in the village knows that he's the best rooster on earth. How do you think I feel when I know he has been waylaid by some *(raises his voice to a shout)* bloody basket! *(turning and addressing the centre of the village in a frenzied call)* It is like losing your own child!

SALOME: Stop shouting, Moses. The neighbours are all looking at us. Keep your voice down, because we are not sure whether he has been stolen or not.

MOSES *(excitedly pointing to various parts of his body):* I tell you he has been stolen. My eyes, my brains, my nose and even my arms and legs tell me that Jeremiah's Horse has been robbed and eaten. Yesterday I saw Noah Kimapu's children wearing long rooster feathers in their hair. I swear they are the same beautiful ones from his tail.

SALOME *(raising her voice now in impatience):* Now you are accusing your third cousin. You should be ashamed of yourself.

MOSES *(shouting angrily):* Shut up woman! How dare you say that to me when I am sorrowing the loss of Jeremiah's Horse. Get out of this house! *(Moves and picks up the broom and chases his wife and children from the house.)* Get out! Get out! Jeremiah's Horse, where are you?

(Stands shaking in anger for a few minutes then suddenly realizes the fact that tomorrow is Sunday and that he is also an apprentice preacher of the village. Groaning he slowly falls to his knees.) Oh! Oh! Oh! What have I done? Please God, forgive me. I did not mean to lose my temper. It was just the wicked spirit of my ancestors who carried me away for a while. Please God, forgive me and don't send your bad angels to visit my gardens.

(Lights fade with the sounds of agonizing groans as if a

soul is bruning in oil.)

SCENE II

Sunday morning inside the village church. The CHURCH WARDEN is parading up and down the aisle which separates the women on the right from the men on the left. He stops in front where the children are and occasionally smacks the knuckles of a child to wake him up. Since the congregation sit on the floor with legs stretched forth and arms propped behind to support, it is not uncommon for children to continually fall backward when sermons are too long, sometimes old folk too.
PAULO, the Mesinari, *is vigorously conducting the singing from the little pulpit in the front and the congregation are singing with passionate devotion. You can see written in their faces that the stimuli for such passion are thoughts of God, of their lovers, of the games after the service, tomorrow's fishing exchange at the coast and even their gardens. If you put your finger against the walls or the tin roof, you can feel the whole building rocking with the fury of a military brass band. The congregation are singing the popular hymn "Jesu Keriso Kalitanya Sogu Kulega" (translated means — "Friend come hear the Horn of Jesus Christ").*

PAULO *(waves the congregation to a stop, opens the Bible, places it on the lectern and motions his flock to bow their heads):* Let us bow our humble heads to get our breath back and to reflect on these words of God. *(flicking the pages obviously and gracefully)* It is written in Matthew V: verses 27 to 30. The Word of God says: *(pause, then in priestly tone)* "You have heard that it was said, do not commit adultery. But now I tell you, anyone who looks at a woman and wants to possess her is guilty of committing adultery with her in his heart. *(A single laugh cracked from the back. The flock all turn*

their heads to the old man who made the noise. The
Mesinari *lets the rumble settle and continues, not*
knowing whether to laugh or to get angry.) So if your
right eye causes you to sin, take it out and throw it
away! It is much better for you to lose a part of your
body than to have your whole body thrown into hell. If
your right hand causes you to sin, cut it off and throw it
away. It is much better for you to lose one of your
limbs than to have your whole body go off to hell."
(slight pause)

CONGREGATION *(in obedient and frightened voices)*:
A-m-e-n.

PAULO: You can lift your heads now. *(Clears his throat and*
pauses for a while) My Dear Brethren, the flock of our
Lord Jesus Christ, today we celebrate this holy day
specially because one of our faithful with the grace of
God is about to become a bearer of God's words. Our
brother Moses Tobudi will give us his first preaching
today. He has struggled for five years as a *Tobalesia* and
God has approved his worthiness. That is why today
Moses will bear the honourable rank as a preacher in our
midst.

(The Mesinari *takes his chair. The congregation murmur*
in anticipation, the children laugh quite loudly as the
boys sitting next to TOPALU and MWAKENA begin
jabbing the two brothers on the side with their elbows.)

CHURCH WARDEN: Stop that! I saw you do it, you
ungrateful little brat! *(Then herding with his stick, he*
removes the main culprit to the very front row.) There!
Sit still. At least the holy words may sink into your
skull if you sit close enough to the Bible and the
preacher! *(The other children murmur in laughter.)*

(MOSES walks seriously up to the pulpit. The
congregation is electrified with expectations of both
success and disaster.)

MOSES *(grasping the lectern firmly as if the stand might just*
run away from him): Brothers and sisters in Christ, and
children: I feel I am not good enough to stand before

you, but somehow I know God wants me to be proud of this great task. We know what our Lord Jesus Christ said about pride — "the first will be last and the last will be first" — so I think we should not be the first to pass judgment on our fellow men. *(Wants to continue but his sudden glance at the children reminds him that he is supposed to give a sermon.)*

Last night as I lay sleeping in my bed, I dreamt a face of a boy, who appeared before me. The face was talking but I could not hear one word from his mouth. Suddenly this common verse that we know so well came into my mind *(gesturing with his hands)* and I began to hear words coming out of the lips of the boy. The sounds of the words were as sweet as the cool evening breeze. What could I do? I knew then that it is God's plan that I should use this verse as the food for my first sermon. Brethren, let us turn to this verse in the holy book.

(He flips the marked page open and in a learned voice he reads) Luke VI: verses 27 to 31 "But I tell you who hear me. Love your enemies, do good to those who hate you, bless those who curse you and pray for those who mistreat you. If anyone hits you on the cheek, let him hit the other one, *(pauses in order to emphasize this sentence)* and when someone takes what is yours, do not ask for it back. Do for others just what you want them to do for you." *(Pauses, closes the book with a bang and looks across the faces of his listeners.)*

I think the message is as clear as our chief's tallest coconut tree that blocks the entrance to the village. Forgiveness, forgiveness is the soil on which love for our neighbours can grow. God's word is that we should forgive one another. *(Pauses and looks upward to the ceiling.)*

You know, I think forgiveness can be the hardest work a man has to go through. Forgiveness must involve two things. First of all the wrong-doer must repent for the bad actions he has committed and secondly the person who is wronged must be willing to forget the losses which were brought upon him. The man who is wronged shows greater love for God if he can prove his worth by forgiving his brother. *(Pause)*

That is why we pray together on Sundays and openly confess our wrongs before our brothers. In this way we learn to forgive our brothers and sisters but also more importantly we know our sins to be cleansed from confessions. *(Pauses and faces the brethren in concluding advice.)*

You see, life is something like a wild boar. It has long tusks and makes such horrible noises that hunters are already scared of it before they even see its back. We are the frightened hunters in the jungle of temptations. Forgiveness is the spark of courage which the hunter needs in order to face up to the deadly attacks of the boar. If we cultivate the habit of forgiving, we can be sure that we are on our way to heaven, where our master is preparing the feast for us.

(The congregation is momentarily hypnotized by such brilliant oratory. Then realizing the fact that it is the end of the apprentice-preacher's sermon, they respond with a loud A-m-e-n.*)*

PAULO *(rising):* I cannot add any more to the words of God as explained by our brother Moses. It is very clear to all of us who are gathered here. I now call on the rest of you faithful to respond to the spirit of the Lord. Let the Lord work through you that you may reveal the messages to the rest. Anyone is now welcome to reveal what is burning in his or her mind. Any confessions to be made, please do not be afraid to confess your sins. We are *all* brothers and sisters in the eyes of our Creator. *(A pause, then an old woman who is a Nakalesia slowly rises to her feet.)*

NAKALESIA *(drawling her words):* I have something biting me inside my chest. Three nights ago I dreamt that a mad dog was chasing me as I was coming back from the gardens. It wanted to bite my mouth and my nose. I was very frightened and dropped the basket of yams that I was carrying. I think this is a way that God is using to show me my sins. Oh God forgive me for using my mouth to gossip about the good name of my daughter-in-law. What I said was all lies. Please God forgive me.

CONGREGATION *(in unison):* A-m-e-n.

NOAH *(rising to his feet and looking in the direction of MOSES, who in return glares at the penitent):* Our brother Moses has spoken the truth about the virtue of forgiveness. Sometimes it is very hard for the wrong-doer to take the first step of admitting his faults, because we are all human beings, we fear what our neighbours will do and think of us. Sometimes we see our neightbours' goods and our desires dance like flames. Who do we blame? The thief or the owner who proudly displays these goods to show what a person that man is? Justice has many sides and I think that if we are going to forgive we should all look at the many sides of any act which is considered a crime. I commend our brother Moses for his honesty and straightforwardness. I think we all have a lesson to learn from him, not only from what he says but from what he does as examples of forgiveness.

(Pauses, then continues in a different tone.)

Three days ago my throat had a wild desire to eat chicken meat. It nearly drove me mad, then suddenly the devil sent a temptation before my eyes. It was our Brother Moses' prized rooster, the Jeremiah's Horse, and . . . *(He is stopped by a sudden thunderous roar from the pulpit.)*

MOSES: So it was you, you bloody basket! I knew it all along and my stupid wife thought I was wrong.

(Leaps down the aisle and fights Noah, all the time yelling out "bloody basket". The whole congregation begin shouting as they attempt to break up the fight. The fight now spreads to the women.)

(Lights fade with shouts and screams from the flock

who are by now heatedly battling each other. Voices yelling: "Have mercy, God! God have mercy! Stop this bloody fight!")

ARTHUR JAWODIMBARI

The Old Man's Reward

A play based on Ferdinand Oyono's novel *The Old Man and the Medal* (Collier Macmillan, 1971).

CHARACTERS

DANUBA	an old man of about sixty
PAINE	his wife
ONJEDE	his cousin
GEROLA	Onjede's wife
KOENA	village constable
DOREI	evangelist
FATHER BILL GRAHAMS	
DISTRICT COMMISSIONER	
ASSISTANT DISTRICT COMMISSIONER	
MINISTER FOR EXTERNAL TERRITORIES	
MIKE SMITH	patrol officer
POLICEMEN	
COUNCILLORS	
EUROPEAN WOMEN	
OTHER EUROPEANS	
HOUSEBOYS	

SCENE I

The lights fade in on DANUBA who sits on a mat yawning. PAINE enters rubbing her eyes and mumbling sleepily.

PAINE: Why are you up so early? Are you planning to go anywhere? A man of your age needs to rest longer.

Every time you are alone you think about Jawo and Mokade.

DANUBA: Don't talk about our sons. They are in God's hands. They died fighting the yellow men and I am proud of them. Come, kneel down beside me and we'll say our prayer. *(They both kneel)* O Iesu Keriso thank you for keeping us safe through this perilous night and for sending your angels to guard us. Help us and guide us in the right footpath so that we do not go astray like other people. Amen.

PAINE: Amen. *(They both sit down on the mat)* Why were you rolling from side to side all through the night? Is anything wrong? Or did you hear any news about your relatives?

DANUBA *(wearily):* Nothing is wrong and I had no bad news at all, but I just could not sleep. Perhaps the *Tauba* is out patrolling. I suspect something terrible is going to happen.

PAINE: But my husband, you have done nothing to worry about the *Tauba's* arrival. Why? Why should the *Tauba* take you to the dark house?

DANUBA: Remember he comes without warning. Go out and sweep the place before you cook some food. *(PAINE gets the broom and starts sweeping. She looks up and sees KOENA coming and runs to DANUBA.)*

PAINE: My husband, what have you done? The Dabuwa man is coming to our place early in the morning.

DANUBA: Our Lord knows the truth, and so it will be revealed to us before long. Don't say anything and hurt yourself with grief. Here he comes. *(KOENA comes closer)* May morning be good to you.

KOENA: And to you too, my beloved old couple.

DANUBA: Come right up here. I see you brought me a message. It is too early for a visit. Sit down and tell us what you have brought. *(KOENA and DANUBA sit on the mat while PAINE sits on the ground)* Speak now, your unusual visit makes my heart beat faster.

KOENA *(coughs):* I went to the district office yesterday to give them the census book. Then I heard your name mentioned there. It was in the mouth of all people. At last the District Commissioner himself came down and asked me if I knew you. Well, to obey government's law and not to sin against God I had to admit that I knew you. He then asked me to tell you to go and see him tomorrow morning. Be careful in your manner. Raise your hand to the level of the right eyebrow, when you enter his office. When answering, say yessa.

PAINE: Why does the *Tauba* want to see Danuba? He has not offended the *Tauba* or disobeyed his laws. He is a friend of the missionaries.

KOENA: Maybe the missionaries want some more of your land. Maybe they want to negotiate it with the government.

DANUBA: Why can't they come straight to me? I gave them three quarters of my land to build their church on. Everything belongs to God and I will give it back to those who are his messengers on earth.

KOENA: I think you won't go to the dark house. But mind your manner! Don't mumble when you talk to the *Tauba*, speak out clear and loud. But I'll be on my way, the sun will be very hot later.

DANUBA: Stay, son, have something to eat before you go.

KOENA: No, I'll go. But remember what I told you. Be at the district office before sunrise! Stay well.

DANUBA: ⎫
PAINE: ⎬ Go well. Our good wishes go with you.

(KOENA goes.)

DANUBA: This is the message that kept me awake last night. I wonder if it is good or bad? Anyway — I can't run away from *Tauba*, so I'll go tomorrow morning.

PAINE: Why can't these white people leave you alone? You gave them your land. Your sons joined the Pacific Islands Battalion and died for the whiteman. And now they want to see you. Before long I will be helpless.

DANUBA: Have faith in our Lord! Remember how God

tested Job; and remember how God planned to save the children of Jacob through Joseph. All these things are the plan of God. *(Enter ONJEDE and GEROIA)* Ah, my cousin and his wife are here. Have they followed the Dabuwa man?

ONJEDE: Cousin, may morning be good to you.

DANUBA: May morning be good to you and your wife too. Come right here and sit down. Surely, morning is good, but I am not in an easy mood. *(ONJEDE and GEROIA sit down.)*

ONJEDE: That's why we are here. I was returning from a hunt, when I met that Dabuwa man. He told me he was coming to deliver your message. So we followed him.

DANUBA: You must have followed him closely, he left only a little while ago.

PAINE: Danuba did not sleep last night. He was rolling from side to side all through the night.

OBJEDE: One whose name is mentioned does not sleep well. But is it good or bad? I am anxious to know.

DANUBA: Cousin, it may be bad. The Dabuwa just told me to see big *Tauba* tomorrow morning at his office.

GEROIA: We were worried about Paine. If the Dabuwa man took you away, who would stay with Paine?

PAINE: No one will. I'll drink the deadly juice of posionous roots if they take him away.

DANUBA: I am glad you'll stay with Paine while I'm away.

ONJEDE: No cousin, I will come with you.

DANUBA: Cousin you must stay. But if I don't return by tomorrow evening, you must bring Paine to the Government station. But let us find something to eat first. We have a long day and night to chat. You women cook some food, while we men go out and look for some betel nuts and mustard leaves.

GEROIA: Onjede, be sure you show your cousin the magic herb of persuasion. It is a powerful herb.

PAINE: Don't stay away too long, because big *Tauba* might send more messengers.

DANUBA: We won't be long.

ONJEDE: We will be back before the food is cooked.
(*Exit ONJEDE and DANUBA.*)

SCENE II

The DISTRICT COMMISSIONER and the ASSISTANT DISTRICT COMMISSIONER sit around the table, talking.

DC: The Minister for External Territories will be here tomorrow. Have all the planters been invited?

ADC: Oh, yes, they've all been told. Some of them will be arriving this afternoon.
(*Enter MIKE SMITH.*)

DC: Ah, Mike. Come in. Take a seat. We were just talking about the Minister's visit.

MIKE: Have the villagers been told to come and stage a sing sing?

ADC: Oh boy, once we pass the word around the whole place will be crowded out with dancers and they will be going on for hours and hours.

DC: The Minister won't have enough time tomorrow to see any dancers. He's just stopping over here to give away that medal. Anyway — he must be bored stiff with all those sing sings by now. It's always the same, isn't it?

MIKE: What's this I hear about old Danuba receiving a medal?

DC: Oh yes. The old fellow is receiving a medal on behalf of his two sons who were killed during the fighting with the Japs. He really deserves it, the old man. I don't know why they didn't give it to him long ago.

ADC: Well, the new policy stresses friendship between the races, multi-racial society and all that. So they start to dig out all these old "deserving" cases.

DC: Well, they could have given him some cash rather than a medal. He's bound to lose it, or drop it in the fire or something.

ADC: By the way, what's the fellow going to wear? He's not

going to meet the Minister in a *sihi* or something, is he?

DC: Thanks for reminding me. Mike, have a look in the store and see if you can find an old coat and a pair of shoes?

ADC: Well, I better be off. I have a court session today.

DC: Oh yes, those drunken New Guineans who beat up a white man in the pub — isn't it? Drop in for a drink in the afternoon!

(DANUBA enters from the right and stands shyly in the corner of the stage near the doorway.)

ADC: See you later. *(The ADC and MIKE leave and make for the door. DANUBA retreats hastily.)*

MIKE: Hey! Don't run away. Come here and tell us what you want.

DANUBA *(saluting):* Me Danuba.

ADC: Are you the old man getting the medal?

DANUBA *(looks puzzled):* Nnno - sssa, I don't know sa, I come to see big *Tauba.*

ADC: You probably come to see the DC about your medal. It's pretty early to see the big *Tauba,* but since you are a great man now, you can see him straight away. Mike, show him in. *(Exit ADC)*

MIKE: Alright, my friend, follow me. *(DANUBA follows MIKE to the DC's office. DANUBA salutes.)*

MIKE: Sir, this is our old friend, Danuba.

DC: Thank you Mike. You go and have a look for some clothes. *(DC extends his hand. DANUBA manages to give a broad smile and he shakes hand. Exit MIKE)* How are you, Danuba?

DANUBA: Thank you, *Tauba,* thank you.

DC: I have an important message for you. The Minister for External Territories who lives in Australia and who is the number one master of Papua New Guinea is coming here tomorrow to give you a medal for your loyal services to the Government. We know that you gave your two sons to defend the country during the war, and your name has reached the ears of the Minister. *(DANUBA stands sullenly)*

But, ehm, take a seat, Danuba, take a seat. *(DANUBA*

tries to grab a chair) No, no, I mean sit down, sit down, Danuba. *(DANUBA sits uncomfortably on the edge of the chair)* Tomorrow we will be celebrating and you will come and join us, together with some of the councillors. You will become famous in your village, Danuba. Everybody will know you as the white man's friend.

DANUBA: Excuse me, sir *Tauba,* is this big big *Tauba* the same one who lives in Konedobu?

DC: No, no, no. This big Tauba is coming all the way from Australia. *(The DC gets up and thrusts his hands in his pockets. He walks around the room just a trifle impatiently)* It will be a great day for you tomorrow, and for all of us. Make sure you come early. You must not keep the big *Tauba* waiting.

DANUBA: Yessa, *Tauba. (Enter MIKE with an oversize coat and a pair of small shoes.)*

DC: Ah, here you are. Now, Danuba. Here are some clothes which you can wear tomorrow. The Government is also giving you a present of some tins of meat, some sticks of tobacco, some biscuits and some toilet paper. And here is a bar of soap — so have a good wash before you come and see the Minister tomorrow. *(He turns to Mike)* Now you better run him down to the village and tell the villagers to come tomorrow for the celebration.

MIKE: All right, sir. Should all the councillors be issued with coats?

DC: O no, forget it. They'll be all right as they are. *(to Danuba)* Now this coat and these shoes are not yours. They belong to the Government. You will return them to the *Kiap* tomorrow after the ceremony. All right?

DANUBA: Yessa, *Tauba.*

DC: Well, there is a car to take you back. Is there anything you want to ask me about?

DANUBA: Yessa, *Tauba.* Will my wife and my people come round to see me get the medal?

DC: Yes, sure. Why not? After all, you will be the big man tomorrow. *(He stretches out his hand. DANUBA grasps it firmly)* And remember to be on time tomorrow.

DANUBA: Yessa, *Tauba*. Thank you *Tauba*. I will come before sunrise!

SCENE III

PAINE, ONJEDE and GEROIA are sitting on the mat. They are talking anxiously in low tones.

PAINE *(sighs):* I wonder what is holding up Danuba? He has been away for the whole day. The sun is about to set and there is no sign of him.

GEROIA: He knows all the footpaths, so he can't lose his way in the bush. That means he must still be at the Government station.

ONJEDE: It is not yet dark. So don't be downhearted. He is probably on his way, maybe some friends asked him to stop and eat with him on the way.

PAINE: He should not stop on the way. He should come straight home to tell us what the *Tauba* said.

ONJEDE: Listen, there is a car coming! *(Car noises. Brakes. Slamming of doors outside.)* What can that be?

MIKE *(outside):* All right Danuba. See you tomorrow.

DANUBA *(outside):* Thank you sa.
(Enter DANUBA, carrying a soap box, a coat and a pair of shoes. They all jump up excitedly.)

PAINE: My husband!

OBJEDE: Danuba!

GEROIA: He is here!

PAINE: What happened?

OBJEDE: Why did the *Tauba* follow you to the village?

GEROIA: This has never happened before!

PAINE: We have been worrying the whole day. Tell us: is it good or bad?

DANUBA: Let me rest first. I am too tired to say anything.

OBJEDE: You women, keep quiet. Let him rest first. If it was something bad he would have said so already.
(DANUBA sits down lazily beside ONJEDE)
Cousin, is it — good, or — bad?

DANUBA: Cousin, it is not bad. I won't go to the dark house after all. But I must go back to the Government station tomorrow.

PAINE: Why do you have to go again?

(Enter KOENA from the right.)

KOENA: May evening be good to you all.

ALL: May evening be good to you too.

KOENA: I saw Danuba arrive in a car. I saw the young *Tauba* driving the car. I came to find out what the big *Tauba* said to him.

PAINE: My husband, did you really come in the white man's car?

DANUBA: Didn't you hear the sound of the car? Yes, I was driven here by the white man. The whites are now my friends.

PAINE: Your friends? My husband, that is impossible. No one is the friend of the white people.

KOENA: Well, is it good or bad.

DANUBA: It is not bad. They told me that the big big *Tauba* who lives across the sea in Australia is coming tomorrow to give me a medal. *(KOENA and ONJEDE whistle and bite their thumbs.)*

GEROIA: Such things have never happened before. My husband's cousin will be a great man among us.

KOENA: When is the big day?

DANUBA: Tomorrow.

PAINE: Will the big *Tauba* send cars to pick us up?

DANUBA: No, we will all have to get up early and walk.

KOENA: All must hear this news! At last one of us is going to be a man. I'll go and tell everybody about it. *(Exit.)*

DANUBA: Fool! He did not wait to hear the whole story.

ONJEDE: And is the white man coming here only in order to give you a medal?

DANUBA: Oh yes! He is coming specially to see me. From now on, I am their friend, and no doubt I will soon go and visit them in their country.

GEROIA *(to PAINE)*: My sister, from now on there will be no more hard work for you. You will eat, drink and

133

sleep all the time. You will ride in the white man's cars.

PAINE: Sister, this is impossible. I can't understand how this came about. I can't believe it.

ONJEDE: If I'm taken to court, I will always tell the *Tauba* that I am Danuba's cousin and then he'll let me go. *(Enter KOENA and DOREI the evangelist.)*

DOREI: May the Lord bless Danuba. May the Lord be with you all. *(DANUBA rises.)*

ALL: May the Lord be with you too.

DOREI: This morning Paine came to church and I assured her that nothing would go wrong. You see now — the Lord always helps.

DANUBA: It is through the Lord God that my name has reached the ear of the big *Tauba*.

DOREI: Let us say a short prayer and thank God.

DANUBA: I was so tired that I forgot to say my prayer. *(They all kneel.)*

DOREI: O God we thank you with all our hearts for giving us our daily bread and meat. We thank you for what you have done for Danuba who will be honoured in our land.

ALL: Amen! *(Crowd of VILLAGERS enters noisily as the prayer ends. They carry drums and they surround DANUBA and dance and sing around him noisily.)*

KOENA: All right, all right! Listen everybody. Tomorrow you must all be at the Government station and as soon as Danuba is given his medal you must all shout together!

(A tremendous shout goes up.)

ALL: Yes!!!!! We will!!!!!

DANUBA: I think the Government may give you some food tomorrow. But now I must try on this coat and these shoes the Government have given me. *(DANUBA tries on the coat.)*

KOENA: You are a truly great man — not like us village constables.

GEROIA: I feel like crying seeing him in that coat.

PAINE: I feel like laughing. The coat's too big for him. He

looks like a small boy in his father's coat. *(The crowd laugh.)*

DANUBA: No, this coat is a new fashion. The whites change their fashion all the time.

PAINE: It looks like old fashion to me — but oversize!

DANUBA: Don't talk too much, otherwise I will go to the station tomorrow without a coat.

KOENA: No no, it fits you. Even though I have been a village constable for five years, I have never worn one. I envy you! *(He giggles.)*

PAINE: Try the shoes. *(DANUBA sits down and tries to fit his feet into the shoes.)*

DOREI: Push your feet in. They're just the right size.

DANUBA: Oh God, these things will give me blisters. *(He just manages to get his feet in.)*

DOREI: Now let us see you walk! *(DANUBA gets up and staggers.)*

PAINE: He waddles like a duck!

DANUBA: I can't walk in these to the station! I'll go barefoot!

ONJEDE: You can't do that. We want you to be properly dressed when you meet the big *Tauba*.

KOENA: I know what to do. I'll fetch some water with those shoes then they'll be soft by tomorrow.

ONJEDE: Put some sand in them, so that the water won't run away quickly. *(Exit KOENA with the shoes.)*

DANUBA: I am tired. Those who wish to stay here can help me to spread the mats on the ground. Those who wish to go home can go now.

ALL: Danuba! Danuba! *(The drumming and singing begins again. They dance round DANUBA and out of the house. Only GEROIA and ONJEDE stay behind, spreading the mats. As the music fades away off stage KOENA enters with the shoes, dripping wet.)*

KOENA: Here you are. You won't feel any pain tomorrow.

DOREI: Goodbye Danuba and don't forget to thank the Lord for his kindness.

SCENE IV

DANUBA stands near the flag pole. An Australian flag over his head. Behind him there is a rope tied, that separates him from the VILLAGERS. To the right, on the verandah of the District Office, the ADC, MIKE, Father BILL GRAHAM and a couple of LADIES are reclining in easy chairs, sipping drinks. DANUBA shows extreme discomfort. He is tired, sweating and badly wants to piss.

ONJEDE: Poor Danuba, he's been standing there for a long time.

KOENA: He's been standing like this since sunrise! Aren't his feet sore in those shoes? He must be sweating under that huge coat.

DOREI: It's a great day for him today, so don't bother about the pain. I'm sure he wants to piss too — but who would bother on such an occasion?

ONJEDE: He must be very thirsty by now. Why can't these white people give him something to drink?

PAINE: Why can't they ask him to sit down with them? His feet must be numb.

DOREI: The big *Tauba* will be here any minute. Danuba has to be ready. Standing there he will gather courage to meet him. None of us know how to meet such big people!

ONJEDE: But he's an old man. Why do they leave him in the sun under that flagpole?

DOREI: That flag is a big symbol for the Government. It is as important to the Government as the cross is to the Christians. He is supposed to show great respect to it.

KOENA: How many medals is he going to get? One for each son who died? *(PAINE breaks out into tears and is led away by GEROIA.)*

DOREI: You shouldn't say such things. Why must you mention her sons now? *(DANUBA looks round, sees PAINE crying. He makes a helpless gesture, then stares*

*straight ahead again. There is a bugle sound. All the
EUROPEANS jump up. The ADC rushes over to
DANUBA.)*

ADC: Danuba, the *Tauba* from Australia is coming.
Remember to stand to attention when he comes.
*(Enter the MINISTER with the DC followed by four
POLICEMEN. He walks over to the European side and
shakes hands with everybody. Laughing cocktail
conversation is being mimed.)*

KOENA: Look! He is a big man with a red face!
*(The MINISTER and the DC stroll over to DANUBA.
The National Anthem is played on a somewhat shaky
trumpet. Everybody stands to attention. DANUBA
salutes.)*

DC: Your Honour, this is Danuba, whom you heard so much
about. He is very loyal to the Administration. His two
sons died fighting the Japanese.

MINISTER *(extends his arm):* Hallo Danuba, how are you.

DANUBA: Thank you *Tauba.*

MINISTER: The Government has heard about your loyalty
and about the heroic death of your sons. I am happy to
award you this medal in the name of the Queen as a
token of our appreciation and as a token of the
continued friendship between our peoples. *(He pins the
medal on DANUBA's chest. They shake hands. A roar
of approval goes up behind DANUBA. The MINISTER
turns to go.)*

KOENA: What, is that all? That was only one medal!

ONJEDE: Shut up!

DC *(clapping his hands):* Listen everybody. We shall celebrate
this important event in the Council Hall. There will be
free drinks and biscuits. Come everybody and listen to
the Minister's speech. *(Exit MINISTER and DC
followed by all the others. DANUBA calls out after
Father Graham.)*

DANUBA: Father, Father!

FATHER GRAHAM *(turns round angrily):* You'll see me
later. I'm in a hurry to get to the Council Hall. Come

and see me tomorrow.

DANUBA: Father, can't you give me a lift to the council hall in your Toyota?

FATHER GRAHAM: All right then, quickly. Hop in the back!

SCENE V

The Council Hall. On a table on the dais, the MINISTER, the DC and OTHER EUROPEANS. On another table, lower down the COUNCILLORS and DANUBA. The crowd on benches.

DANUBA: Hei! Here, my glass is empty. *(The HOUSEBOYS look away)* You boys, my glass is empty.

FIRST COUNCILLOR: You better be quiet now. We are going to toast. You can have more drink later. *(Everyone raises his glass to toast except DANUBA who stares at his empty glass.)*

SECOND COUNCILLOR: What have you done with your beer? You shouldn't gulp it down like that!

FIRST COUNCILLOR: Don't listen to him. It's a big day for you, so you must drink more than your stomach can hold. You see all those bottles over there? We must drink all of it before we go.

SECOND COUNCILLOR: Here, here, my glass is empty! Come on! We're not drinking anything.

FIRST COUNCILLOR: You people are drinking faster than the white men. *(The ADC casts some angry glances at them, but they are too drunk to notice.)*

DANUBA *(gets up)*: Come on now, bring drinks! Why are you serving those white people first? They haven't finished their glasses yet.

FIRST COUNCILLOR *(pulls him down)*: Sit down. Don't make so much noise. They are looking at us now.

DC *(raises his hand)*: Everyone keep quiet. His honour is going to speak. *(DANUBA gets up trying to catch another drink — the COUNCILLORS pull him down.)*

DC: All quiet please.

MINISTER: The District Commissioner, Ladies and Gentlemen. I wish to thank you for your wonderful hospitality. I have enjoyed myself thoroughly. I am particularly happy to notice the cordial relations that exist here between Australians and New Guineans. I hope that this friendship will intensify in years to come. I would like to congratulate our friend Danuba for being such a loyal man to the Administration and I hope everyone will follow in his footsteps. We shall never forget the fact that his sons died fighting at the side of their Australian brothers. It is my sincere wish that with the help of loyal people like Danuba we shall build this country into a happy multi-racial community. Thank you all. *(By now DANUBA is asleep, but he is startled when the people applaud. He tries to get up.)*

FIRST COUNCILLOR: Sit down my friend, the party is nearly over.

DANUBA: I want to talk to the big *Tauba*. I want to thank him for coming all the way to give me the medal.

FIRST COUNCILLOR: Sit down my friend. You are drunk, sit down.

DC: Let him speak. I think he's got something to say.

DANUBA *(steps forward):* I thank you big big *Tauba* for coming all the way from Australia for giving me my medal. I thank the big *Tauba* and the other white men for providing us with all these expensive drinks. I thought I wouldn't have enough — but I have had more than I have ever had the chance to drink before. It is good to see the beginning of this new friendship between the white people and the New Guineans. I hope it continues till we will all know each other very well. *(Applause)* Now to return the hospitality we have received here today, I want to ask the big *Tauba* to come with me to my house now and share the pig that I am killing for the feast. Since we are now drinking together, we must eat together too. *(Applause)* Thank you very much.

(The MINISTER whispers in the DC's ear.)

DC: Thank you Danuba. His Honour says that he appreciates your invitation very much. He would love to share your meal with you, but unfortunately he has some urgent business in Moresby and so he will have to leave almost at once. However, he says, that whenever you come to Canberra, he will be very pleased to see you and to entertain you there. *(DANUBA sits down. His friends support him)* Now I want everyone to rise to his feet, because His Honour is leaving. Three cheers for His Honour.

ALL: Hip hip, hurray, hip hip hurray, hip hip hurray!
(DANUBA sinks to the floor and dozes off.)

DC: Now you may finish the drinks, but I want everybody out of here before dark.
(The whites leave.)

SECOND COUNCILLOR: Our friend is drunk.

FIRST COUNCILLOR: You're drunk yourself. You are making a hell of a noise.

SECOND COUNCILLOR: Wake your friend, he is sleeping like a log.

FIRST COUNCILLOR: Let him sleep. He is very tired. *(He removes DANUBA's medal and takes a close look at it)* Ah, this is called Victoria Cross. It is very beautiful.

SECOND COUNCILLOR: Let me see it. *(FIRST COUNCILLOR gives it to him. Everybody crowds round making a lot of noise.)*

MAN: Let me see it, let me see it.

SECOND COUNCILLOR: Hey, you dropped it!

MAN: You dropped it yourself.

SECOND COUNCILLOR: No you did!

FIRST COUNCILLOR: Let me pick it up! Make room there, I say make room! *(A big fight ensues. Everybody beating everybody. Suddenly the POLICE enter, led by MIKE.)*

MIKE: That's enough! You've all had enough. So get home quick. So everybody buggeroff!
(They chase out COUNCILLORS and DANUBA remains lying on the floor. The lights fade slowly.

Darkness. A pause.
Enter two POLICEMEN, shining a torch.)

FIRST POLICEMAN: Ah! Here's one of them. Asleep.

SECOND POLICEMAN: Wake him up! He maybe pretending.

(FIRST POLICEMAN wakes him up.)

FIRST POLICEMAN: What are you doing here — everybody has gone home!

SECOND POLICEMAN: What are you doing here? What are you up to?

DANUBA: I — I want to sleep. *(He falls back drunkenly.)*

FIRST POLICEMAN: Hei! Stand up, when you speak to a policeman! What's your name?

DANUBA: I am Da — da — nu — I am — oh my head!

SECOND POLICEMAN *(manhandling him):* I think you'd better spend the night in the cell.

DANUBA: Leave me alone! Don't you know I am the friend of the white man?

FIRST POLICEMAN: Ha! Ha! Listen to that. Come on. We'll lock you up: drunk and disorderly!

DANUBA: I want to sleep.

SECOND POLICEMAN: Yes, but not here. You'll sleep in the dark house. Come on old fellow.

(They drag him out.)

SCENE VI

MIKE sits at a table in his office. Enter a POLICEMAN who salutes.

MIKE: What's up Borege?

FIRST POLICEMAN: Sir, I arrested a man last night for being drunk and disorderly. He spent the night in the cell.

MIKE: All right, let's see him.

FIRST POLICEMAN: Sir! *(He salutes and leaves promptly.)*

MIKE: Ah, well. I guess we had too much grog flowing last night. *(The two POLICEMEN drag in DANUBA)* Hey,

Danuba! Is that you? What happened to your medal? *(DANUBA looks down on the floor)* I knew you would be losing it before long, but not that soon! *(laughs)* O well, never mind. Have a smoke! *(DANUBA refuses to take it.)*

SECOND POLICEMAN: Don't make *Tauba* angry, take it.

MIKE: Leave him alone. Just shut up. *(DANUBA takes the cigarette and smokes it)* Well, old fellow. You can go home — never mind — but don't get drunk again will you? *(DANUBA moves to the door)*

Hi, come back Danuba! I nearly forgot about your coat! Are you trying to run away with it? Now come on, take off your coat and the shoes. They belong to the Government. Borege, bring a piece of calico for Danuba. Only one.

FIRST POLICEMAN: Sir! *(He salutes and leaves. DANUBA removes coat and shoes and tries to hand them to MIKE, who steps back with ill disguised disgust.)*

MIKE: Sergeant, take those things off him! Get them washed before returning them to the store. *(FIRST POLICEMAN returns with the calico)* Danuba, wear that piece of calico over your shorts. *(DANUBA looks at it)* Go on! Wrap it round your waist. *(SECOND POLICEMAN laughs)*

O.K., old fellow! You can go home, now.

(DANUBA walks out carrying the piece of calico.)

SCENE VII

DANUBA's house, the VILLAGERS sit around lazily. The men sit chewing betelnut. The women are rolling stringbags.

GEROIA: My sister, your husband must be having a good time. He is probably the first man to sleep in a white man's house.

PAINE: My sister, I am worrying about him. If he slept in the white man's house, he would have been here by now. I fear he got lost in the night.

GEROIA: My sister, the white man might bring him in their car. They will bring him home after the midday meal. He is not a small boy to get lost on the way.

ONJEDE: Women, can't you talk about anything else? If you talk about my cousin, he will have a bad time, or he will knock his foot on his way home.

PAINE: But why hasn't he come home? All the councillors returned last night.

ONJEDE: My cousin's wife, councillors are nothing. They are not men. My cousin is a man!

KOENA: He should have asked his wife to come and enjoy the good things with him in the white man's house.

PAINE: Danuba is not like other men. He makes sure that I share what he eats.

(DANUBA enters, limping. He looks tired and sick.)

KOENA: Danuba! He looks sick! *(PAINE gets up and collapses. GEROIA supports her.)*

ONJEDE: Come, let us carry him in. The spirits of his sons must have led him in the bush. They must have dumped him in the mud. Look, he is very dirty. *(They run up to carry him.)*

GEROIA: He looks very sick. Find out if he is possessed by the spirits . . .

ONJEDE: My cousin, are you sick? Where did you sleep? How did you get this mud all over you? Did someone attack you on the way home? *(DANUBA is silent.)*

KOENA: Maybe the whiteman gave him too much to eat and to drink. He must have been falling all the way from the Government station. Why didn't they bring him in their car?

ONJEDE: Maybe the road was too muddy for the car to get through. Cousin, tell us about your white friends.

DANUBA: Cousin, you don't know the ways of these white men. They tell you they are your friends, then they shut you in their dark house. They will never treat you as a man. *(PAINE stops weeping and looks at DANUBA surprised.)*

143

KOENA: Did you run away from their dark house? Is that how you got mud all over your body?

ONJEDE: Why did they put you in the dark house?

DANUBA: Why? Do the white men need a reason? *(PAINE and GEROIA move closer.)*

ONJEDE: Where is your coat? Did they take it back from you?

DANUBA: Cousin, don't trust the white man to give you anything. They dress you up, they call you a man, then they ask you to return everything.

KOENA: Did you bring your medal?

DANUBA: I am an old man, leave me alone. Don't ask me any more questions. Someone bring me a cup of water. *(GEROIA goes off to fetch water.)*

ONJEDE *(shaking his head):* Cousin, you shouldn't have gone to the Government station. Maybe the white people were just looking for such an old man like you to play their tricks.

DANUBA: Cousin, if I hadn't gone I would still be in their dark house.

KOENA: Maybe God was not on his side.

DANUBA *(angrily):* Go out! Don't preach to me. Preach to someone younger than me. *(GEROIA returns with a cup of water. DANUBA drinks it slowly. Enter DOREI with Bible and prayer book.)*

DOREI: God be with you all. May the Lord bless Danuba's house.

DANUBA: Get yourself blessed first. Leave me. I don't want to see your face.

DOREI: What's wrong with Danuba, the most faithful Christian in the village? The bad spirit must have entered his mind. *(He retreats.)* I'll read you an extract from the book of Job.

DANUBA: Read it to yourself. Keep your God. He is the white man's God. I gave all my land to him — now see how he allows his people to mock me.

DOREI: Take courage. Have you not got the medal? Is that not a big reward for all your suffering?

ONJEDE: Let's leave him now. He looks very tired. Dorei, come on, we must leave him alone. *(Everyone makes for the door. ONJEDE turns back again and squats by DANUBA.)* My cousin, is there anything at all I can do for you?

DANUBA: What can you do for me? My land is gone. My sons are dead. I have been humiliated. Go . . . go . . . I feel tired . . . I am an old . . .

PAINE *(very sadly and very quietly)*: Oh my husband, what have you done; you have sold our two sons for a medal. *Lights fade*

Glossary

aiesade	coming *(Mailu)*
aioni	goodbye *(mailu)*
avesa	woman *(Mailu)*
bagarap	damaged, hurt, out of order, tired *(Pidgin)*
baimbai	will, shall *(Pidgin)*
balus	aeroplane *(Pidgin)*
bedira	type of tree providing durable wood for building posts *(Mailu)*
berete	belt *(Pidgin)*
B.P.	Burns Philp Trading Company
damorea	traditional mourning song *(Mailu)*
dubu	large ceremonial platform *(Mailu)*
ekalesia	of the Protestant church *(Mailu/Motu)*
em i sik	he is sick *(Pidgin)*
em tasol	that's it *(Pidgin)*
godagoda	expression of excitement or satisfaction used on striking a target accurately *(Mailu)*
goniga	species of palm tree *(Mailu)*
Iesu Keriso	Jesus Christ *(Mailu/Motu)*
kaikai	food *(Pidgin)*
kanaka	originally *man (Fijian)*. Now a derisive form of address *(Pidgin)*
kapurika	cucumber *(Mailu)*
kaukau	sweet potato *(Pidgin)*
kiap	patrol officer *(Pidgin)*
kukurai	someone designated to represent the government, though not necessarily a natural leader; traditionally chief of the village *(Pidgin)*

kunai   grass, especially of grasslands; also *Imperata arundinacea,* alang-alang or sword grass *(Pidgin)*

laplap   clothes; cloth *(Pidgin)*

madava   a productive garden; see *oioi* and *tako (Mailu)*

masta   master, white man, European, ruler *(Pidgin)*

mesinari   pastors of the village *(Pidgin)*

milo   a brand of chocolate drink *(English)*

mi tink somting i bagarap na yu sinaut   I thought you shouted because something was wrong *(Pidgin)*

mi tok   I said *(Pidgin)*

modiu   Mailu hunting game no longer played *(Mailu)*

mumu   earth oven; also something cooked in an earth oven*(Pidgin)*

nakimi   brother in law *(Motu)*

namo   good *(Motu)*

namo herea   very good *(Motu)*

namotamota poki namotamota   dust to dust *(New Hebrides)*

nipa   *Nipa fruticans;* a type of palm *(botanical)*

ogogami   poor *(Motu)*

oioi   a cleared but uncultivated garden; see *madava* and *tako (Mailu)*

olsem wanem   what's up? *(Pidgin)*

pitpit   *Saccharum spontaneum;* wild sugar cane *(Pidgin)*

piripous   trousers, shorts *(Motu/Mailu)*

seia   seat *(Pidgin)*

skel   ration *(Pidgin)*

S.T.C.   Steamships Trading Company

supe   God *(New Hebrides)*

superi   dear God, term used in prayers *(New Hebrides)*

tako	cultivated food garden; see *oioi* and *madava* *(Mailu)*
tapa	cloth made from beaten bark (from *Polynesia)*
taraka	truck *(Pidgin)*
taro	*Colocasia;* an edible root (from *Fijian)*
tasol	see *em tasol (Pidgin)*
tauba, taubada	man of importance, "big man", now used simply as "white man" *(Pidgin)*
tete	term used by children for mother *(New Hebrides)*
tikes	tickets *(Pidgin)*
tobalesia	devoted Christians *(Trobriand)*
toguya	preachers *(Trobriand)*
tok	talk *(Pidgin)*
toligalega	special disciples *(Trobriand)*
wantok	a person who speaks your language, someone on whom you have have claims, especially kinship claims; friend; fellow countryman *(Pidgin)*
Yu go we?	Where are you going *(Pidgin)*
Yu pela i wokim gut na baimbai yu kisim skel bilong yu. Yu harim?	If you work well, you will get your rations. Understand? *(Pidgin)*
Yu Pela ol frends na wantoks *Yumi lukluk insait nau long yumi yet!!!*	Friends and fellow countrymen, it is time we examined ourselves!!! *(Pidgin)*

Notes on Contributors

Sergeant Bagita, who came from the Milne Bay District, died at the age of sixty-nine in 1972. He was a retired sergeant of the Papuan Constabulary, and held the MBE.

Ulli Beier was born in Germany in 1922 and studied literature in England. He went to Nigeria in 1950 where he lectured at University College, Ibadan. As editor of the literary magazine *Black Orpheus* and founder of the Mbari Clubs of Ibadan and Oshogbo, he acted as a catalyst in the publication of Nigerian writers. He taught at the University of Papua and New Guinea 1969-71 and was founding editor of the *Papua Pocket Poets* series, of *Kovave,* a journal of New Guinea literature, and general editor of Jacaranda Press's Pacific Writing series. In 1972 he became Director of African Studies at the University of Ife, Nigeria.

Wauru Degoba is a student at Goroka Teachers College. He comes from the Western Highlands. He is working on a book of tales about Chimbu life.

Benjamin Evara is an Arts student at the University of Papua New Guinea. He comes from the Purari Delta.

Leo Hannett was born in 1941 on Nissan Island in the Bougainville District. He is a graduate of the University of Papua New Guinea and is currently at the East-West Centre at the University of Hawaii researching political developments in the British Solomon Islands Protectorate. His play *The Ungrateful Daughter* is in *Five New Guinea Plays* (Jacaranda, Brisbane, 1971) and he has written in *Overland, Kovave* and other journals.

Lazarus Hwekmarin was born in 1952 at Kwagwie Yongoru

149

in the East Sepik District. He is an Arts student at the University of Papua New Guinea. His poems have appeared in *Kovave* and *Papua Pocket Poets*.

Brother Allain Jaria comes from Woitape in the Central District. He is studying for the priesthood at M.S.C. Novitiate, Vunapau, New Britain. His poems have appeared in *Kovave, Overland* etc.

Arthur Jawodimbari was born in 1949 at Beporo near Popondetta in the Northern District. He is a graduate of the University of Papua New Guinea. He is the author of six plays, of which *Cargo* is in *Five New Guinea Plays,* and has written for *Kovave, New Guinea Writing,* etc. At present he is attending a postgraduate course in drama at the University of Ife, Nigeria.

John Kadiba was born in 1946 on the island of Mailu in the Central District. After graduating from the University of Papua New Guinea he worked as a tutor at Raronga Theological College, Kerevat. He is now studying for a divinity degree at the University of Queensland. He has written for *Kovave, New Guinea Writing* and the Australian Broadcasting Commission. Kumalau Tawali's play *Manki Masta* based on one of his stories is in *Five New Guinea Plays.*

Pokwari Kale is a law student at the University of Papua New Guinea.

John Kasaipwalova was born at Yalumgwa village on Kiriwina in the Trobriand Islands, and has left an Arts course at the University of Papua New Guinea to work with grass roots political and economic movements in the Trobriand Islands. He has written three plays, edited an issue of *Kovave,* and is founding editor of the poster poem series published by the Centre for Creative Arts, Port Moresby.

Albert Maori Kiki is Minister for Lands in Papua New Guinea. He comes from Orokolo in the Gulf District. He was founding national secretary of the Pangu Pati and a leading trade unionist. He is the author of an autobiography *Kiki: Ten Thousand Years in a Lifetime* (Cheshire, Melbourne; Pall

Mall, London, 1968) and, with Ulli Beier, *Hohao* (Nelson, Melbourne, 1972). He has received a Commonwealth Literary Fund fellowship to work on a third book.

Bede Dus Mapan was born in 1947 at Mendi, and comes from the Southern Highlands. He is an Arts student at the University of Papua New Guinea. His Neo-Melanesian (Pidgin) poem "O Meri Wantok" launched the Centre for Creative Arts poster poem series. His first collection of poems is scheduled to appear in *Papua Pocket Poets*.

Meokoro Opa was born in the Gulf District in 1950. He studies economics at the University of Papua New Guinea. His poems and stories have appeared in *Kovave, New Guinea Writing,* and *Overland*.

Jacob Simet is a Tolai Student from Matupit near Rabaul in the East New Britain District. He was born in 1952. Formerly at the Lae Institute of Technology, he now attends the University of Papua New Guinea. His writing has been published in *Kovave, New Guinea Writing, Overland* etc.

Russell Soaba was born in 1950 at Tototo in the Milne Bay District. He is an Arts student at the University of Papua New Guinea. His stories and poems have appeared in *Kovave, Youth Writes Again,* (Reed, 1971) etc.

Kumalau Tawali was born in 1946 at Tawi village on a small island south of Manus. An Arts graduate of the University of Papua New Guinea, he has published poems and stories in *Kovave, New Guinea Writing, Overland, Poetry Australia* and the *Post-Courier*. His play *Manki Masta* ("Houseboy") based on a story by John Kadiba, is in *Five New Guinea Plays*. A collection of his poems, *Signs in the Sky,* was published in *Papua Pocket Poets* in 1970. He was briefly editorial adviser of the journal *New Guinea Writing*. Kumalau Tawali is now in Europe with Moral Rearmament.

Lynda Thomas was born on Kiriwina in the Trobriand Islands in 1950. She studied Arts at the University of Papua New Guinea, and was involved in Women's Liberation. She has published poems in *Kovave,* and a short story in *New Guinea Writing*.

151

Maurice Thompson was born at Pele in the New Hebrides in 1945. His poems and other stories have appeared in *Kovave* and *Poetry Australia*. He is a graduate of the University of Papua New Guinea.

John Waiko was born in 1941 at Tabara near Popondetta in the Northern District. He is a graduate of the University of Papua New Guinea, and is currently doing postgraduate studies at the University of London School of Oriental and African Studies. His play *The Unexpected Hawk* is in *Five New Guinea Plays* and he has been working on a collection of Binadere folk tales. He has written for *Kovave, New Guinea Writing, Journal of the Papua New Guinea Society*, etc.